The Pathology of Power

Books by Norman Cousins

ALBERT SCHWEITZER'S MISSION: HEALING AND PEACE

THE HEALING HEART

THE WORDS OF ALBERT SCHWEITZER

ANATOMY OF AN ILLNESS AS PERCEIVED BY THE PATIENT

HUMAN OPTIONS

DR. SCHWEITZER OF LAMBARÉNÉ

THE IMPROBABLE TRIUMVIRATE

THE PHYSICIAN IN LITERATURE

WHO SPEAKS FOR MAN?

THE CELEBRATION OF LIFE

PRESENT TENSE

IN PLACE OF FOLLY

MODERN MAN IS OBSOLETE

THE GOOD INHERITANCE

"IN GOD WE TRUST": THE RELIGIOUS BELIEFS AND IDEAS OF
THE AMERICAN FOUNDING FATHERS

The Pathology of Power

by

NORMAN COUSINS

Foreword by
GEORGE F. KENNAN

W · W · NORTON & COMPANY
New York · London

Published simultaneously in Canada by Penguin Books Canada Ltd., 2801 John
Steet, Markham, Ontario L3R 1B4.
Printed in the United States of America.

The text of this book is composed in Times Roman, with
display type in Friz Quadrata. Composition and
manufacturing by The Haddon Craftsmen Inc.
Book design by Jacques Chazaud.

First Edition

Library of Congress Cataloging-in-Publication Data

Cousins, Norman.
The pathology of power.

Includes index.
1. Power (Social sciences) I. Title.
JC330.C65 1987   303.3'3   86–21658

ISBN 0-393-02378-8

W. W. Norton & Company, Inc., 500 Fifth Avenue, New York, N.Y. 10110
W. W. Norton & Company Ltd., 37 Great Russell Street, London WC1B 3NU

1 2 3 4 5 6 7 8 9 0

Dedication

To everyone who feels in his bones the truth of Jefferson's belief that government must never be allowed to become a shelter for deception or arbitrary power; to everyone who believes that peace with justice in today's world is still possible and is everyone's business; and to everyone who has taken pains to communicate with public officials urging better policies than are routinely offered.

Contents

Foreword

By **George F. Kennan**

When the first nuclear weapon was exploded over Hiroshima, and in the years immediately following, a number of weighty and impressive voices could be heard, pointing out that the emergence of destructive power of this magnitude invalidated the greater part of traditional thinking about the relationship of war to national policy and calling for the adoption of a new mindset—a new way of looking at things, one based on the recognition that war was no longer a rational option for great industrial powers and that other means would have to be found to resolve the conflicts of interest that would always be bound to arise among them.

In some instances, these demands came from the great intellects of the day. Those of Albert Einstein and Bertrand Russell are well known, and have been frequently republished. Less well known are those of certain of the military leaders, particularly those mentioned in this volume—Generals Douglas MacArthur and Dwight Eisenhower (others, notably Lord Mountbatten, might also have been cited). All of these men perceived the suicidal quality of the nuclear weapon and the danger in allowing it to become the basis of defense postures and the object of international competition. All of them spoke with a great sense of urgency. All went to their deaths hoping, surely, that their warnings would not fall on deaf ears and that a new generation of leaders would recognize that we were all living in a world of new political-strategic realities and would draw the necessary conclusions.

Unfortunately, this has not happened. For thirty years past these warning voices have been disregarded in every conceivable respect. There has been no new mindset. There has been no recognition of the revolutionary uniqueness of the weapons of mass destruction— no recognition of their sterility as weapons, no recognition of the dangers of their unlimited development. On the contrary, the nuclear explosive has come to be treated as just another weapon, vastly superior to others, of course, in the capacity for indiscriminate destruction, but subject to the same rules and conventions that had governed conventional weaponry and its uses in past ages. The suicidal quality of these devices has been ignored. They have been made subject to the primitive assumption that the value of a weapon is simply proportionate to its destructiveness, and that the more you have of any weapon, in relation to the similar holdings of your adversary, the more secure you are. Coherent political purpose has been lost sight of behind the calculations of sheer destructibility and the fascination of numbers. And all those psychological distortions that had been allowed to accompany armed conflict in the pre-nuclear age have come to be applied to the competition in the development of this form of weaponry: the same exaggerations of enemy iniquity and capabilities, the same excesses of chauvinistic self-righteousness, the same thirst for unconditional surrender and total victory, the same mad assumptions that out of vast destruction and suffering there could come something called "victory," and that this would ensure the emergence of a better world. People have gone on, in other words, behaving as though this were 1916 instead of 1986 and as though the nuclear weapon were only some new species of artillery. This was, of course, precisely what the Einsteins and the Eisenhowers and the others had tried to warn about.

We can see today the result of this rejection. After the passage of some thirty years, the security of this country has not been improved; never, in fact, was it more endangered than it is now. The nuclear arsenals have grown to absurd and monstrous dimensions

—far beyond anything that even the most sanguine military logic could justify. Their very numbers have made them a potential danger to the world environment. The proliferation of nuclear weaponry into other hands, some of them far less responsible than those of the original nuclear powers, goes on apace, as it was bound to do, so long as the superpowers placed no restrictions upon their own cultivation of it. And to this whole process—the nightmarish growth of the arsenals and the dangerous proliferation of the nuclear capability—there is no limit in sight. So far as we, the civilian laymen, are allowed to see, the process is supposed to go on indefinitely, into a future where every sort of outcome is conceivable except a happy one —a future so remote as to reach into a time when those who are now promoting it will be long gone; and there can be no telling in whose hands this awesome responsibility will then rest.

And it is not only the external effects of this dreadful progression that we must take account of. Hand in hand with it has gone, and must continue to go, a serious weakening of American society and an impairment of American democracy. It has led to the emergence of a military-industrial establishment of such dimensions that it has become the greatest single factor in our economic life, overshadowing the peaceful and constructive elements of the American economy and in some respects encroaching on them and replacing them. It is an establishment largely outside the perimeter of democratic control, as Eisenhower so clearly perceived it might be. Constituting as it now does the greatest single purchaser in the American market, with all the power that implies, anchored in long-term contractual obligations that defy the normal annual budgetary discretion of Congress, its tentacles now reaching into almost every congressional district and distorting the electoral situations wherever they reach, this military-industrial establishment has become a veritable addiction of American society—an addiction from which American society could no longer free itself without the most severe withdrawal pains. Were the Soviet Union to sink tomorrow under the waters of the ocean, the American military-industrial complex would have to go on, substantially unchanged, until some other adversary could be invented. Anything else would be an unacceptable shock to the American economy. The truth of the matter is that the greater portion of American society that lies outside the defense establishment is rapidly falling in a position resembling that of much of civilian society in northern Europe toward the end of the Thirty Years' War: reduced to trailing behind the armies as camp-followers, hoping to live off the remnants from the military stores and kitchens.

So vast a peacetime defense establishment has demanded, of course, as a counterpart indispensable to its rationale, an adversary proportionate to it—proportionate in its alleged iniquity, in the presumed intensity of its hostility, and in the immensity of the armed power with which it was supposed to confront us. This counterpart was found, in the form of the Soviet Union; and the forbidding image has been assiduously built up and nurtured, as it had to be, over the course of several decades. It was not that the reality of Soviet power provided no sustenance at all for the development of this image. The Soviet Union did indeed present problems for the statesmen of the West. The apparently inordinate size of its armed forces; its postwar position astride the eastern half of the continent; its fading but still perceptible world-revolutionary rhetoric; the forbidding aspect of the Stalin regime, surviving down to 1953; its obsession with secrecy; the anxious isolation of its people from normal contact with the outside world; and the persistent presence within its political-military establishment of an element no less militarized in its thinking and no less inclined to think in terms of some ultimate military showdown than some of those who confronted it on our side of the line: all these were real phenomena. What was wrong was not that they should be taken into account, as they had to be. What was wrong was that they became subject, at the hands of those who cultivated this image, to a regime of oversimplification, exaggeration, misinterpretation, and propagandistic distortion that had the cumulative effect of turning a serious but not unmanageable problem into what appeared to many people to be a hopeless, insoluble one —insoluble, that is, other than by some sort of apolcalyptic military denouement. So assiduously was this image cultivated that it became with the years part of the stock-in-trade of the electronic media,

subject to all their propensities for overdramatization and vulgariza-
tion, pounded into the public mind day after day by one visual
impression after the other, until the wicked Russian became the
common villain of the spy-story and the common nightmare of
children. Behind this curtain of self-delusion and self-hypnosis the
real image of Soviet society retired farther and farther into the
shadows, remote from the vision and the attention of the wider
reaches of American society. It was thus that a discriminating relationship between two of the world's greatest societies also fell victim
to those same tendencies of thought—that same militarization, that
same ignoring of the realities of the time, that same inability to relate
military considerations realistically to the other concerns of our
society—against which the warnings had been uttered.

This great distortion of vision was of course never the entire
picture. The attitudes it produced have been flanked at every turn
by other ones—more critically thoughtful, more penetrating and
realistic. But these two tendencies, most unfortunately, have never
been reconciled in official American thinking. They have been allowed to exist side by side; and such is the nature of the American
political system that it has proven politically expedient for established authority not to try to reconcile them; for this would have
implied an intellectual responsibility too heavy for most of those in
political life. It was easier to try to appease both bodies of thought
—one out of the righthand pocket, the other out of the lefthand
one—while trying to let each think it was having its way. The result
has been an attitude toward the Soviet Union that can only be
described as half war and half peace. Summit meetings, the façade
of normal diplomatic relations, cultural and scientific exchange programs, a little trade (where demanded by some domestic-political
lobby), and a modicum of peaceful tourism: these have been permitted to proceed with at least a pretense of normality. But back of them
all the machinery of the great military establishment, and above all
of the related intelligence and internal security systems, has ground
along in its own ponderous, relentless way, largely remote from
political observation or control, basing itself daily on working assumptions that could not have been much different had one known

with a certainty that all-out war with the Soviet Union was both inevitable and impending. To which fact has to be added the recognition, so amply supported by historical example, that to believe a war to be inevitable, and to act accordingly, is the best way to make it so.

The conclusion to which all this points is one of great gravity, but it is inescapable. The problem posed by the discovery and development of nuclear weaponry has proved to be one too large for the normal political system of this country. The qualities of mind required—one cannot say for its solution (that goes too far) but for coping with it in ways that do not spell utter disaster—are not ones encouraged by active participation in the political process. Intellectual leadership as opposed to the catering to mass reaction; the long view as opposed to the short one; the readiness to accept immediate hardship and to take the immediate risks with a view to averting much greater ones in the distant future; the insistence on tackling the schizophrenia that now prevails in American attitudes toward Russia and working out an attitude that will have both soundness and consistency—these things are not for the legislator with another election looming imminently before him; they are not for the official caught up in the vast networks of modern governmental bureaucracies and subservient to the primitive assumptions on which these latter usually operate; they are not for the political leader daily measuring his popularity by the reactions of the television screens and the opinion polls, harried hourly by a thousand different duties and problems of his office, and beholden in countless ways to the impressive posture and the effective slogan for the success of his effort. One can conceive of help coming, in these circumstances, only from some sort of a permanent outside body advisory to the president—a body of men and women (and not too many of them) made wise by natural aptitude and long experience in the ways of the world, people wholly disengaged (at least at this stage of their careers) from the political process, people enjoying sufficient public respect and confidence so that their views would carry weight—a body of senior statesmen, in short, capable of supplying the president with precisely that sort of thoughtful and measured advice in the great matters of war and peace that he is unlikely to get from the men normally around him in the turmoil of his office.

One must hope that there will at long last be some movement in that direction, as thoughtful people have repeatedly urged. But it would be unrealistic to suppose that anything of this sort could mature in the near future. In the meantime, we will remain dependent on the lonely individual thinker who has come to possess, by one means or another, the delicate but not wholly trivial power of the pen. To this category of persons Norman Cousins eminently belongs, as he has belonged for so many years; and it is this ineffable power, frail and yet not always so frail, that his book possesses.

When Mr. Cousins invited me to introduce this book, he observed that I might not be in agreement with all of it. This is true; but the areas of disagreement are secondary, the areas of agreement —decisive. It reflects the wisdom of an honest and courageous spirit, accumulated over many years of involvement with public affairs as editor, educator, and commentator. Were there to be a body of senior statesmen such as the one I have suggested, Mr. Cousins would be a charter member of it. For this, and for the depth of the concern that he shares with so many other thoughtful people, his book deserves the attention of the serious reader.

Prescript

CONFESSION: This book is written in a mood of indignation and sadness over the way new attachments to power are distorting the traditions of freedom in America.

When first I read reports about military misspending and waste, as evidenced by $435 hammers and $15,000 sofas, I thought it unfair and short-sighted to allow a few aberrant items to serve as a basis for judging anything as far-reaching and complicated as a program for protecting the national security. But when these reports began to mount and involve entire weapons systems and, even more important, the way decisions were being made about military contracts, it became apparent that the term "national security" was being used to disguise the massive transfer of public funds to private sources. Ironically and inevitably, the safety and security of the nation are being weakened and jeopardized in the process. It is fair to ask whether people who have demonstrated they cannot be trusted to safeguard the wealth and resources of the American people should be trusted to safeguard the national security.

These feelings are intensified, if anything, because of the vantage point from which this book is written. For the past eight years, I have been stationed in a medical school. Part of my duties involves working directly with seriously ill patients, attempting to relieve their panic by bolstering their will to live and giving them confidence in their doctors and their own resources. I belong to an establishment in which a large number of men and women are probing for better ways of eradicating and combatting disease. They are aided by all sorts of new technological marvels for aiding diagnosis and treatment. With each passing day, however, the grim sense of paradox increases. With a single official command, more suffering can be let loose on the world than has been recorded so far in all the annals of medicine. Medical researchers work constantly to create new antibiotics and other medications for combatting infections. But the United States and Soviet Union, in their own research laboratories, are creating strains of bacteriological organisms for use in warfare, far beyond the reach of any known antibiotics. We must contend with the fact that the main threat to the health of human beings today is not the absence of medical attention but the nature of national foreign policies.

The fact of a collective madness has yet to register on our consciousness. The obsession with total power; the manufacture and stockpiling of cataclysmic weapons far beyond any conceivable need; the relentless quest for superiority; the comparative casualness with which the suicidal nature of such force is viewed; the seeming acquiescence in the drift toward a man-made holocaust—all these are symptoms of a pervasive insanity. The application of psychiatric standards permits no conclusion other than that the governments have been gripped by a deep psychosis that is working its way, as in deep-rooted diseases, toward a hideous culmination.

Let us suppose that two men who regard each other as enemies are in the same lifeboat. Each feels insecure about the designs of the other. Each possesses a drill. Now let us further suppose that each man feels the best way of protecting himself against the other is to threaten to drill a bigger hole in his end of the boat than the other is capable of drilling at his end. The psychotic nature of such an episode is readily apparent, yet this is the essential nature of the nuclear dilemma in the modern world. Any rational analysis of this predicament would indicate that the cause of mutual survival would dominate the policies of governments. Yet the major emphasis seems to be on drilling bigger holes in the common lifeboat.

It is too easy to point the finger and say the collective madness in the world today resides in one place. The problem goes beyond any single nation or person and has its origins in the rapid movement of history that has made the world a single geographic unit characterized more by interaction than interdependency; more by the primacy of the national interest than the primacy of the human interest; more by anarchy and temper than organization and order. The need to convert the geographic unit into a functional unit is the dominant need and challenge in our time. This book seeks to expound on that challenge.

One more note: It would be a gross error to suppose that this book is anti-military. The chapters on Gen. Dwight D. Eisenhower and Gen. Douglas MacArthur, as well as the references to Adm. William D. Leahy, Gen. George C. Marshall, and Gen. David Jones, should dispel any notion that I have inadequate regard for the role of the military in a free society. The late Gen. Donald Armstrong, chief of U.S. Ordnance during World War II, and a good friend, was for me a strong example of a military man who also knew that military power must not be allowed to become an end in itself or the means by which the wealth and resources of the American people could be appropriated or exploited.

In any case, as this book seeks to make clear, the central meaning of the atomic age is that there is no defense except peace. That message should be a mandate for the American future even as it should serve as the unifying principle for our dealings with the rest of the world.

Acknowledgments

The term "acknowledgments," customarily used to recognize aid to an author, does not do justice to the persons who helped with this book. The word "collaborators" is more to the point. I had the advantage of several collaborators, beginning with Jean Anderson, who is my editorial and research assistant in much of my work at UCLA. Ping Ho, also of UCLA, has collaborated on several chapters, most particularly the one dealing with "Star Wars." Hallowell Bowser, a former colleague on the editorial staff of *The Saturday Review,* collaborated on the chapters dealing with the historical background, weapons waste, and demonstrated abuse. Adm. Gene La Rocque, Dina Rasor, and the staff of Senator Charles Grassley provided documentary materials. An account of their work in the general field covered by this book is described in the chapter "Whistle-Blowers." I am eager, too, to thank Bob Adams and the Washington bureau staff of the *St. Louis Post-Dispatch* for materials from their series on General Dynamics; Ernest Fitzgerald, also discussed in "Whistle-Blowers," for moral support and a clear sense of direction; and Gar Alperovitz, for basic materials on the decision to drop the atomic bomb. Susan Schiefelbein applied her extraordinary editorial talents to the copy checking of the final manuscript. Janet Thomas provided careful research assistance, and help with the footnotes.

"Collaborators" correctly implies creative involvement but it is not to be construed as a sharing of responsibility for errors or misstatements, all of which are chargeable solely to the author.

I am especially grateful to Ambassador Kennan for his introductory comments. It is inevitable that anyone writing about the dangers and abuses of unlimited military spending will be exposed to the criticism of minimizing or ignoring the Soviet Union. No American today has had a more extended opportunity to study the Soviet Union at first hand than George Kennan; no American has a wider knowledge of the nature of Soviet policies, actions, and intentions. His concern that American power is not being used in the best interests of the American people cannot be set aside in any assessment of a program aimed at creating general security.

STYLE: One of the perennial problems confronting authors is represented by the fact that they recognize an obligation to back up their statements with specific references, but footnotes tend to be messy and cumbersome and slow down the movement of ideas. In order to deal with the need without incurring the liabilities, this book deals with documentation in descriptive form in the appendix, citing chapters and pages to facilitate ready reference.

The
Pathology
of Power

1

The Pathology of Power

This book is about power—how it is perceived; how it is used; its illusions and realities; its benefits and dangers. What confronts the American people as they approach the twenty-first century is the truth of one of the best-known axioms on human behavior: "Power tends to corrupt; absolute power corrupts absolutely."

Author of this eight-word distillation of human experience is John Emerich Edward Dalberg, better known as Lord Acton (1834–1902). Lord Acton wrote copiously on the French Revolution, but none of his books had the impact of a single line he wrote in a letter to an ecclesiastical friend about the tendencies of power. He recognized that nations and civilizations fell into decline—not so much because they were powerless but because of their inability to use their power wisely.

Connected to the tendency of power to corrupt are yet other tendencies that emerge from the pages of the historians:

- The tendency of power to drive intelligence underground;
- The tendency of power to become a theology, admitting no other gods before it;
- The tendency of power to distort and damage the traditions and institutions it was designed to protect;

• The tendency of power to create a language of its own, making other forms of communication incoherent and irrelevant;

• The tendency of power to spawn imitators, leading to volatile competition;

• The tendency of power to set the stage for its own use.

All these tendencies, in varying degrees, are observable in almost every breakdown in history. Thucydides' history of the wars that drained the lifeblood of ancient Greece; Polybius' account of Macedonian errors; Gibbon's study of Rome's ascendancy and its slide from the center of the historical stage; the scores of books on Hitlerian might and disaster—all these works bear witness to the inability of highly organized societies to understand the complexities and perils of their power.

The attachment to total power in our time not only has not served the purposes of national security but threatens to bring about a basic change in the kind of balanced relationship between government and people that is the central feature in the political architecture of the American Constitution-makers. No aspect of this threat is more apparent than the way genuine national security requirements have been allowed to serve as the occasion for an assault on the wealth of the American people. The chapters that follow summarize the reports of public and private investigators—reports documenting the loss amounting to hundreds of billions of dollars, through waste, bribery, kickbacks, circumvention of competitive bidding, flawed weapons systems, and sheer incompetence in the military program.

Few government scandals in American history begin to compare with the enormity of these disclosures. Indeed, the very size and extent of the scandals represent a barrier to effective prosecution or correction. Even greater than the economic dangers inherent in a national debt that will exceed one thousand billion dollars are the political, social, and military implications of the policies that lead to the debt. The fact that the present generation does not fully feel the impact of the accumulated national debt does not mean that the penalties can be deferred forever. The money owed by the government has to be repaid in some form. Traditionally, governments have avoided bankruptcy by promoting policies that cheapen the value of the currency so that the numerical amount of what is owed is respected while the value amount is sharply decreased. In America's case, the result will be depleted value of savings, insurance, and social security—apart from the damaging effects on education, medical services, and the quality of life in general.

The largest single item in the skyrocketing national debt is military spending. Yet one thing must be recognized and emphasized. Any national deficit, however great, is worth the cost and risk if it genuinely promotes the national security. Where the life of the nation is concerned, the size of the national debt is secondary. But when a substantial part of that debt is the result of an underlying situation of misspending and incompetence, the national security becomes endangered even as the quality of life of the American people is undermined.

The mishandling of military power is not unconnected to the exponential increases in the destructiveness of weaponry—or the limitations it imposes on use. The decision to use the atomic bomb did not take fully into account the social, moral, and philosophical implications of nuclear power at the end of the Second World War. The failure to comprehend these implications may be where America took a wrong turning in its perception of the uses of military power. The use of nuclear explosives on Hiroshima and Nagasaki may have been the beginning of a false reliance on unworkable power as the basis of national security.

As the leading nuclear scientists at the time feared, the decision to use atomic explosives bypassed many of the long-range factors affecting the nation's future. The next chapter of this book details the background of that decision. Incontrovertible evidence exists, including President Truman's personal diary and Defense Department documents, showing that the war could have ended without the use of the atomic bomb. Hiroshima, therefore, is an essential starting point for the scrutiny of America's relationship to total power since the end of the Second World War.

In the years following Hiroshima, the U.S. continued to manu-

facture nuclear bombs beyond any conceivable need. Our installations turned out nuclear explosives at the rate of seven to eight a day,
month after month, year after year. By the mid-eighties it was
estimated that the United States had stockpiled more than 30,000
nuclear bombs, even though Robert McNamara, secretary of
defense in the administration of John F. Kennedy, estimated at
the time that 400 such explosives were more than enough for any
predictable military purpose. We were to reach a point where
the nuclear accumulation contained more destructive force in TNT
equivalent than could be carried by a train of freight cars 4,000
miles long.

Nothing manufactured in the world today is in as great abun-
dance as destructive force. The United States and the Soviet Union,
between them, have accumulated enough nuclear force to approximate 1,200 pounds of dynamite for every human being in the world.
The world does not have 1,200 pounds of food or any of the other
necessities of life in reserve for every human being. There is a point
at which accumulation becomes addiction, and a point at which
addiction becomes disease. The stockpiling has become an end in
itself, separated from practical reality, and a substitution of fantasy
for security. The pathological pursuit of power by the major nations
permits no conclusion other than that they have been seized by a
madness, the potential lethality of which eclipses any epidemic' ever
recorded.

The Soviet Union has matched the United States stride for stride
in nuclear capability. The mythology of numbers rather than a
rational plan for mutual survival has defined the relationship of the
superpowers. The main change produced by nuclear weapons is that
national security depends on the control of force in the world rather
than on the pursuit of force. For if the force is used, America would
be in total jeopardy—not just from the assaults of an enemy but from
the devastating effects on the conditions of life itself. Yet the attachment to nuclear power has become so great that resistance to control
is dominant in policy, except for the one shining achievement of a
partial test ban during the Kennedy administration.

Underlying the military and ideological problems involved in the confrontation between the United States and the Soviet Union are profound moral issues. The most important of these moral issues has been inherent in nuclear weapons since the first bomb was exploded. The issue has not been addressed. It is the inevitable product of the fact that the two superpowers cannot war against each other without also warring against the whole of the human race. Nuclear explosives, if used, will have devastating effects on people with whom the U.S. and the USSR have no quarrel. Whether we are talking about the darkened skies resulting from the updraft of debris produced by nuclear war, or about the radioactive garbage carried by clouds, spilling their poisons on lands far removed from the battle zones, or about epidemics that will range across continents, the fact remains that nuclear conflict is a declaration of war on the conditions that sustain human life. An ironic aspect of life in the latter part of the twentieth century is the way power becomes transformed into powerlessness in contact with high technology. The ability to create and exercise power has not been accompanied by the ability to govern its effects.

It may not be within the reach of the present generation of Americans to create global sanity. But it is certainly within our reach to bring rational considerations to bear in the operations of our own government. Beyond that must be the hope that rational leadership might encourage sanity elsewhere.

There is no dispute, no problem, no grievance between our two societies that can justify such an assault on humankind. It is difficult, indeed, to think of any arrogance in history that begins to compare to national policies that seek security through measures which, if used, could make large portions of our planet uninhabitable.

It is not particularly helpful for either of our societies to blame the other. What matters is not what they assert in their relationship, but how, speaking and acting together, they propose to organize the peace. The common aim should be not just to abolish nuclear weapons but to abolish war itself.

Do the two countries have a peace plan to put before the world? What is their plan for common security? How do they propose to make the World Court truly functional? Two countries cannot be policemen to the world. The attempt to cope with terrorism, for example, requires multilateral approaches. Even without respect to violent confrontation, the large nations, just in the exercise of power, put other nations in jeopardy. The operation of nuclear power plants, for example, carries potential hazards that are not easily controlled. Whenever and wherever human beings interact with complicated machinery and processes, errors are inevitable. We have reached a point where the life of entire societies has become utterly dependent on error-free technology. Between 1960 and 1986, the world experienced fifteen major accidents in the manufacture of nuclear power. The most serious of these accidents occurred in 1986 in Chernobyl, in the Soviet Union, when graphite fire caused release of large quantities of radioactivity, carried uncontrollably by the winds far from the site of the explosion.

Similarly, the failure of a U.S. space shuttle early in 1986, with loss of life to all aboard, points to the precarious and intricate technology that is basic to the war capability of the U.S. and the USSR The world is connected in every way except through institutions capable of controlling power and its effects.

There are times in the life of a nation when only power can safeguard it or serve it. But there is never a time when the limitations of power don't have to be recognized and respected, nor ever a time when non-military strength isn't essential for developing the potentialities of a nation and its people. The present danger is not so much that we may fall behind in the competition for superior weaponry as that the power we mount may not fit our needs and may jeopardize the very freedom we seek to protect.

Next to the gift of life itself, freedom is the highest prize this planet has to offer. This philosophical belief became institutionalized in the design for a nation in 1787. The validity and force of that design are demonstrated by the fact that no major nation can point to a longer life under the same form of government than can the United States. But if freedom is the ultimate prize, then the need to nurture it and serve it may well be the ultimate ordeal. The purpose of this book is to show that one of the main dangers to freedom in our time may be the inability to control and use wisely the power created for the purpose of confronting and combatting external threats, real though they may be.

No sure-fire formula for national security has ever been devised. Yet history is not altogether barren as a guide. It teaches us that security has to function for the community of nations or it will function for none. It teaches us that common dangers and common needs must serve as the basis for common institutions or agencies. It teaches us that anarchy is destructive of both freedom and peace. It teaches us that the only alternative to anarchy is law. It teaches us that there is no substitute for reasoned, morally imaginative leadership in meeting day-to-day problems and in the anticipation of problems to come—whether at home or abroad. It teaches us that a healthy society generates national strength.

Disarmament by itself does not create national security, as the history of the 1930s demonstrated. Europe was exposed to the aggression of Nazi Germany because of the assumption by many nations, including the United States, that arms reduction alone could set the stage for genuine peace. The memories of Nazism, its march to power, and its near dominion over more than a billion human beings are too recent to require sermons on the dangers of unpreparedness in the modern world.

The lessons of the 1930s, however, may not be an adequate guide to the problems of the closing years of the twentieth century. Preparedness today requires far broader concepts than it did a generation ago. Moreover, preparedness in terms of sheer force invites its own dangers. In the words of President Eisenhower, there is danger in collecting power far beyond one's needs.

There are related dangers.

There is danger in allowing the military to have an unreasonably large part in decision-making in matters concerning the life of the nation, all the way from domestic economic policy to foreign policy.

There is danger in upsetting or bypassing the checks and balances that safeguard the resources of the American people.

There is danger in creating an open channel between the weapons makers and the U.S. Treasury.

There is danger in allowing the groups producing the weapons to have a strong voice in deciding what weapons are to be produced and in what quantities.

There is danger in making the national security synonymous with the personal security of those who benefit from military spending.

There is danger in creating a military welfare state.

Finally, there is danger that our legacy to future generations of Americans will be a nation economically devastated, depleted of resources, shorn of its traditional freedoms.

These dangers are not inexorable, nor are they beyond control. The kind of progress within reach of Americans, once these dangers are turned back, is incalculable. But, first, history must be consulted and values reassessed. Pathology must be identified and the conditions of creative health systematically understood and applied.

2

The Misperception of Power

I n early July 1945, Gen. Dwight D. Eisenhower, commander of the American military forces in Europe, went to Antwerp. There he met with President Harry S Truman, Secretary of State James F. Byrnes, and Secretary of War Henry L. Stimson, who were en route to Potsdam for a meeting with Prime Minister Winston Churchill and Premier Josef Stalin to discuss the variety of problems left by the defeat of Germany. High on the agenda was the continuing war against Japan.

In *Crusade in Europe,* Eisenhower wrote that he first learned of the successful test of an atomic bomb from Secretary Stimson, who was "tremendously relieved, for he had apparently followed the development with intense interest and felt a keen sense of responsibility for the amount of money and resources that had been devoted to it. I expressed the hope that we would never have to use such a thing against any enemy because I disliked seeing the United States take the lead in introducing into war something as horrible and destructive as this new weapon was described to be. Moreover, I mistakenly had some faint hope that if we never used the weapon in war other nations might remain ignorant of the fact that the problem of nuclear fission had been solved."

Eisenhower enlarged on this account in *Mandate for Change,* saying he told Stimson that he questioned the wisdom of using the bomb. He could tell from Stimson's general mood of elation that "vigorous assent" was expected.

"During [Stimson's] recitation of the relevant facts, I had been conscious of a feeling of depression and so I voiced to him my grave misgivings, first on the basis of my belief that Japan was already defeated and that dropping the bomb was completely unnecessary, and secondly because I thought that our country should avoid shocking world opinion by the use of a weapon whose employment was, I thought, no longer mandatory as a measure to save American lives. It was my belief that Japan was, at that very moment, seeking some way to surrender with a minimum loss of face. The Secretary was deeply perturbed by my attitude, almost angrily refuting the reasons I gave for my quick conclusions."

Eisenhower's statement that Japan was on the verge of collapse is supported by the testimony of America's other military leaders, as recorded in government archives. These documents also show that the U.S. Joint Chiefs of Staff believed it would not have been necessary to carry out the planned invasion. Moreover, President Truman's own diary, inaccessible for many years, contains the statement that just the entry of the Soviet Union into the war, scheduled for August 15, 1945, would have been enough to bring about Japanese surrender. Yet President Truman, in reporting to the American people about his decision to use the atomic bomb, unequivocally declared that Japan was far from defeated at the time and that, were it not for the atomic bomb, hundreds of thousands of American lives would probably have been lost in the invasion.

Obviously, both assertions cannot be true. The president's private journal and the military records attest that Japanese surrender was near; the president's public statements say the opposite. One thing is certain: No one who lived through the Second World War will ever forget the sense of joyous relief that swept over America on August 6, 1945, when the president declared that the United States had dropped an atomic bomb on Hiroshima. The sense of relief was especially real to many thousands of American soldiers who were in troopships en route to Japan, or who were in America or Europe after the collapse of Germany in May 1945 and who were waiting to be sent to Japan.

What the American public had no way of knowing at the time was that most of America's military leaders were opposed to the decision to drop the bomb, believing, as Eisenhower's memoirs emphasized, that neither the bomb nor an invasion was necessary to defeat Japan.

Perhaps the most definitive of the source materials is a report prepared by the Department of Defense dated September 1955 titled "The Entry of the Soviet Union into the War Against Japan: Military Plans, 1941–1945." The report was prepared in response to inquiries from Congress and reviewed the full sequence of events from the day after Japan's attack on Pearl Harbor, December 7, 1941, to the capitulation of Japan on August 10, 1945.

The first entry of the report refers to a conversation between President Franklin D. Roosevelt and Soviet Ambassador Maxim M. Litvinov on December 8, 1941, in which the president inquired about Soviet intentions with respect to the war against Japan. FDR recognized that the U.S. would have to fight on two fronts. Was the Soviet Union prepared to do the same? Litvinov replied that the USSR would remain neutral for the time being.

The report goes on to say that the Soviet decision to remain neutral was discussed at meetings between British and American chiefs of staff in the early weeks after Pearl Harbor. It was agreed that priority had to be given to the defeat of Germany and that "her defeat was the key to victory" in the war. It was also agreed that "only the minimum of force necessary for the safeguarding of vital interests in other theaters should be diverted from operations against Germany."

Periodically, however, according to this Department of Defense document, the matter of Soviet involvement in the Far East came up in U.S. strategy discussions. On March 4, 1942, in a message to the Joint Chiefs of Staff, President Roosevelt reiterated his belief in the strategic desirability of Soviet involvement. The Joint Chiefs concurred in their reply, saying ". . . it is respectfully suggested that the president may care to initiate steps with the Soviet Union looking toward an agreement which would permit complete military collaboration with the USSR."

On December 10, 1941, Chief of Staff Gen. George C. Marshall received a cable from Gen. Douglas MacArthur urging efforts to bring the Soviet Union into the war. MacArthur said that "definite information available here shows that entry of Russia is enemy's greatest fear . . . Golden opportunity exists for a master stroke while the enemy is engaged in over-extended initial war efforts." General Marshall's cabled reply, dated December 15, 1941, assured General MacArthur that his views had been conveyed to the President.

According to the Defense Department report, Soviet participation in the war against Japan was dubious in 1942 and through most of 1943. At the Casablanca Conference of January 1943, President Roosevelt, Prime Minister Churchill, and General de Gaulle emphasized a central strategy aimed at first defeating Germany and then finishing off Japan. On August 6, 1943, in an "Estimate of the Enemy Situation," the Joint Chiefs expressed the belief that "Russia is likely to intervene in the war against Japan at some stage, but not before the German threat to her has been removed. After that, she will make her decision in the light of her own interests and she will intervene only when she reckons that Japan can be defeated at small cost to her."

In October 1943, the president appointed W. Averell Harriman as Ambassador to the Soviet Union. The messages to and from Harriman emphasized the importance of Soviet involvement in the war. Harriman made use of every opportunity to press his views on the Soviet leaders. An encouraging development occurred on October 30, 1943, when, during private conversations at a Kremlin dinner, Foreign Minister Vyacheslav M. Molotov and Andrei Vishinski indicated that the Soviet Union would join the United States in the war against Japan once Germany was defeated.

This impression was strengthened in subsequent months. So much so, in fact, that U.S. military chiefs involved themselves in detailed planning for an invasion of Japan, the chances for success of which would be enhanced by a Soviet attack on Japanese-occupied Manchuria.

At the Teheran Conference in November and December of 1943, Premier Stalin told the U.S. what it was waiting to hear; namely, that he was ready to pledge the full participation of the Soviet Union in the war against Japan. In particular, the Soviet Union agreed to invade Manchuria, synchronizing its plans with U.S. action. The U.S. Joint Chiefs proceeded to develop their plans for combined operations with the Soviet Union. The projected invasion of Japan involved a two-pronged assault—one, an amphibious assault on Kyushu and, second, "a decisive stroke against the industrial heart of Japan by means of an amphibious attack through the Tokyo plain assisted by continued pressure from Kyushu."

In preparing for this invasion, the president asked the various military commanders for their estimates of possible American casualties in the assault on Kyushu. These estimates ranged from 30,000 to 200,000 in the early phases. General MacArthur said the great variable was the extent of the Soviet involvement in Manchuria. The greater the Soviet force, the less formidable the resistance in Kyushu and therefore the fewer the American casualties.

On June 11, 1944, Ambassador Harriman cabled the account of his interview with Premier Stalin the previous evening. The two men had gone into great detail on matters covering Soviet military strategy and tactics in the war against Japan.

During the summer of 1944, according to the Defense Department report, the tide of battle in the Far East began to swing to the United States. On September 23, 1944, Stalin asked Harriman whether the United States preferred to defeat Japan without Soviet assistance. Harriman assured Stalin that "Russian participation was desired." Stalin replied, according to Harriman, that "he was somewhat surprised that, after the assurance he had given at Teheran, we [the U.S.] were not taking into account in our planning the participation of Russia and he appeared anxious to know specifically what role we would want Russia to play. He gave every indication of being ready and willing to cooperate but did not want to be an uninvited participant."

President Roosevelt, on September 28, 1944, sent a dispatch instructing Harriman to reassure Stalin that he, FDR, "at no time entertained any doubts whatever in regard to the Teheran agreement about Pacific campaign." Then, on October 14, the president cabled Marshal Stalin: "I want to restate to you how completely I accept the assurances which you have given us on this point [the war against Japan]. Our three countries are waging a successful war against Germany and we can surely join together with no less success in crushing a nation that I am sure in my heart is as great an enemy of Russia as she is of ours."

Within a few months, however, eagerness by U.S. military planners to have the Soviet Union enter the war dimmed markedly. A notation in the Department of Defense report said that the "campaigns of the fall of 1944 were bringing United States forces to the edge of Japan's inner zone of defense." By November 1944, a planning paper for the Joint Chiefs of Staff said that Soviet participation, which had been thought desirable to hasten the unconditional surrender of Japan, was no longer considered essential. "Throughout current war planning there is implicit conviction that the defeat of Japan may be accomplished without Russian participation in the war."

When President Roosevelt went to Yalta in early February 1945, he was given unequivocal assurance by Stalin that Russia would enter the war against Japan approximately three months after the defeat of Germany. Stalin said he would need that much time to move his forces across Europe and Siberia. Left open were the political terms of Soviet intervention and the military problems involved in coordinating Soviet operations with U.S. planning.

After several days, these questions were addressed at Yalta. The *status quo* in Outer Mongolia would be maintained. Russia's previous rights in Manchuria would be restored. Dairen would be internationalized. Southern Sakhalin would be returned. The Kuriles would be annexed to Russia.

On the military side at Yalta, planning proceeded for joint military operations in the Pacific theater. The U.S. was given access to aviation bases in the Komsomolsk-Nikolaevsk region, and preliminary arrangements were made for weather stations in Russian controlled territory.

On March 8, 1945, Washington received from a Col. Paul L. Freeman, Jr., a summary statement of General MacArthur's views concerning planning for the invasion of Japan. "He emphatically stated that we must not invade Japan proper *unless* [italics ours] the Russian army is previously committed to action in Manchuria," Colonel Freeman reported.

In general, joint planning operations with the Soviet Union got bogged down in the weeks after Yalta. The general atmosphere in the relations between the two countries was not enhanced by developments in Europe, especially with respect to the status of the liberated countries in Eastern Europe and the repatriation of U.S. prisoners freed by the Soviet Army.

Franklin D. Roosevelt died on April 12, 1945; Harry S Truman became president, by which time the deteriorating situation not just of Germany in the West but of Japan in the East created the need for new "assessments." The Department of Defense report said the Joint Chiefs now pondered "the question of whether or not an invasion of the Japanese home islands was actually necessary." A corollary, of course, was the need to "reconsider the value of the Soviet contribution to the effort." By April 16, a report to the Joint Chiefs stated that "military collaboration with the Soviet Union was no longer vital to the United States." On April 24, the Joint Chiefs cancelled plans for use of the Siberian air base. On the same day, it was decided that "Soviet entry into the war was no longer considered necessary" to bring about victory. The Joint Chiefs also recommended to the president that a declaration of intent be delivered to Japan urging the creation of a new government for the purpose of signing a surrender agreement.

After the collapse of Germany on May 7, 1945, the Joint Chiefs of Staff questioned the feasibility of the demand for Japan's "unconditional surrender." "Unless a definition of unconditional surrender can be given which is acceptable to the Japanese, there is no alternative to annihilation and no prospect that the threat of absolute defeat will bring about capitulation."

The collapse of Germany also created the need to anticipate postwar problems. Accordingly, Prime Minister Winston Churchill and President Harry S Truman met with Marshal Stalin at Potsdam in July 1945. In preparation for this conference, Harry Hopkins, who had served as special emissary and trouble shooter, was sent to Moscow where he received assurances that the Soviet Union was firmly committed to entering the war, deploying its troops on the Manchurian border by August 8. Hopkins also reported that Stalin favored a unified and stable China and proposed that China be given control of all of Manchuria.

A key point in Harry Hopkins' report to President Truman was that "Japan is doomed and the Japanese know it." By way of underlining this point, Hopkins said that "certain elements in Japan are putting out peace feelers. Therefore, we should consider together our joint attitudes and act in concert about the surrender of Japan."

Hopkins said that "Stalin expects that Russia will share in the actual occupation of Japan and wants an agreement about zones of occupation."

On June 14, 1945, the Joint Chiefs of Staff asked the Pacific commanders to prepare for sudden Japanese surrender, even though November 1 had earlier been specified as target date for the invasion of Kyushu.

Adm. William Leahy, who occupied the post of top military aide to the president, raised questions at a White House meeting about the policy of unconditional surrender. He feared our insistence on the policy would "result only in making the Japanese desperate and would increase our casualty lists." He saw no necessity for such a policy. President Truman replied that the policy of unconditional surrender was necessary in terms of American public opinion.

At the same meeting, Adm. Ernest King reflected the growing opinion among the American military when he said that the Russians "were not indispensable," and he had no doubt that "we could handle it alone."

Even before President Truman left for Potsdam, the deteriorating military situation of Japan further strengthened the view that

Russian entry into the war was undesirable. U.S. intelligence sources reported that the Japanese Navy had "been reduced to the size of a small and unbalanced task force, the Japanese Air Force was limited to suicide tactics, and thus the Japanese Army . . . retained little, if any, strategic mobility and was exposed to increasing supply shortages."

The same U.S. intelligence reports said that the "Japanese ruling groups are aware of the desperate military situation and are increasingly desirous of a compromise peace . . . We believe that a considerable portion of the Japanese population now consider absolute military defeat to be probable . . . An entry of the Soviet Union into the war would finally convince the Japanese of the inevitability of complete defeat."

The reports went on to raise questions about the feasibility of unconditional surrender and indicated that a change in the American position, allowing the Japanese to keep their emperor, might accelerate the peace process.

Not long after President Truman arrived in Potsdam on July 16, 1945, Premier Stalin showed him a copy of a message received from the Japanese ambassador in Moscow saying that the Emperor would like to send Prince Fumimaro Konoye to the Kremlin for the purpose of exploring possibilities of ending the war. Stalin said he had not replied to the message.

The discussions at Potsdam included detailed plans for the invasion of Kyushu, set for November 1945. The major agreements:

1. Radio stations would be set up in Petropavlovsk on Kamchatka for transmitting weather data in accordance with President Truman's request, although the Soviet Union preferred to use its own personnel at the stations;

2. Separate zones of naval and air operations were to be set up for each country in the Sea of Japan;

3. The boundary lines between operational zones of the U.S. and USSR air forces in Korea and Manchuria were fixed;

4. Liaison officers for the joint operations were identified;

5. Ports and airfields for ships and planes were designated.

Originally, the date set for the Russian entry was August 8, 1945. At Potsdam, the date was extended to August 15. U.S. policymakers became convinced of the need to end the war before that date. This required prompt and unconditional surrender. There was obviously not enough time to get into peace negotiations with Japan and conclude the war before Russian involvement.

As Robert J. Donovan wrote in *Conflict and Crisis: The Presidency of Harry S. Truman, 1945–1948,* news on July 16, 1945, of the successful test of the atomic bomb in New Mexico had "changed the minds of the United States delegation [at Potsdam] about wanting to have the Soviets in on the kill in Asia." Donovan quoted Secretary of War Stimson as saying that "the news from Alamogordo [about the successful test of an atomic explosion] . . . made it clear to the Americans that further diplomatic efforts to bring the Russians into the Pacific war were largely pointless." Donovan added that "Truman suddenly lost interest in the date when the Soviets planned to march in Manchuria."

In view of the long series of efforts to bring the Russians into the war in the Far East, there appeared to be no way to keep them out at this stage. In any event, the sudden loss of interest by the Americans in joint planning for the Russian entry did not go unnoticed by the Russians, judging from the fact that on July 29 Molotov said the Soviet Union was waiting for a "formal" request to enter the war. Truman, no longer eager about this prospect, told Molotov that it would be desirable to create a formula "under which Soviet intervention would spring from obligations to the United Nations." That same day, Truman signed the order for the use of the atomic bomb. A supplementary order specified that the bomb was not to be used while Truman was still at Potsdam.

At this point, we turn to President Truman's own journal, beginning with his diary entries at the Potsdam Conference.

For thirty-four years, the pages of President Truman's diary relating to the events of Potsdam were apparently lost. What had happened was that Presidential Press Secretary Charles G. Ross had borrowed sheets from the diary, intending to write about the Potsdam Conference. He never finished the account and the diary sheets were returned to the White House where they were misfiled, coming to light only in 1979.

The notations in Truman's diary during the last two weeks of July 1945 tell of his belief that the moment Russia came into the war, Japan would collapse. Just the fact that Russia was poised to fight would be decisive. Two entries are relevant here. Under the date of July 17, 1945, Truman reported his conversation with Premier Stalin. "Most of the big points are settled," he wrote. "He'll be in the Jap war on August 15 . . . Fini Japs when that comes about." This point was underlined the next day when he wrote in his diary, "Believe Japs will fold before Russia comes in."

In view of Truman's own certainty that the war would end within a short time, his own later public statement about the need for an invasion calls for careful scrutiny. Not just Truman's own diary but interviews with Secretary of State James F. Byrnes show that Truman became convinced at Potsdam of the need to knock out Japan before the Soviet entry into the war. The big question was not whether Japan was on the verge of defeat but whether defeat could be brought about before August 15, 1945. In any case, Truman's own diary contradicts his later statements about Japan's lack of interest in peace negotiations. As stated earlier, his Potsdam diary entry for July 18, 1945, revealed that Moscow had received a cable "from Jap Emperor asking for peace."

The big change in the president's eagerness to involve the Soviet Union in the war against Japan came on July 25, 1945, reflected in this entry: "We have discovered the most terrible bomb in the history of the world." Then came a reference which has largely gone unnoticed in the history of the period. The president said he directed Secretary of War Henry L. Stimson not to use the bomb against civilians. He specifically ordered that the bombing be confined to military objectives. "Even if the Japs are savage, ruthless, merciless and fanatic," he wrote, "we as the leader of the world for the common welfare cannot drop the terrible bomb on the old capital or the new [Kyoto or Tokyo]." The president's journal revealed he ordered that a warning to Japan about the bomb be issued, "asking the Japs to surrender and save lives."

This reference to the president's intention to issue a warning about the atomic bomb meant that Japan would have the responsibility to decide whether it would be used in the war. Yet the president changed his mind, not just about a warning but about the use of the nuclear bomb on civilians, directly contradicting an earlier order to Secretary Stimson. Why?

An interview given by Secretary of State James F. Byrnes to *U.S. News and World Report* for August 15, 1960, may provide the answer. An unequivocal question was put to Secretary Byrnes: "Did we want to drop the bomb as soon as possible in order to finish the war before Russia got in?"

Secretary Byrnes's reply: "Of course, we were anxious to get the war over as soon as possible."

The interviewer persisted: "Was there a feeling of urgency to end the war in the Pacific before the Russians became too deeply involved?"

Secretary Byrnes's reply was unambiguous: "We wanted to get through the Japanese phase of the war before the Russians came in."

The article also referred to the diaries of James Forrestal in which the former secretary of the navy wrote: "Talked with Byrnes, now at Potsdam. Byrnes said he was most anxious to get the Japanese affair over with before the Russians got in . . ."

Leo Szilard, the noted physicist who figured prominently in persuading President Roosevelt to proceed with the attempt to develop a nuclear explosive, was also interviewed for the same issue of *U.S. News and World Report.* He discussed his own conversations with Secretary Byrnes, repeating the same points attributed directly to the secretary, adding that he was told by Secretary Byrnes that he and the President believed the use of the bomb on a live target, before the war was over, was necessary to make an impression on the Russians and to make them "more manageable" following the war.

It is interesting to note that the special issue of *U.S. News and World Report* devoted to the decision to drop the bomb also featured a direct statement by Edward Teller that the use of the atom bomb "was a mistake." Like General Marshall, Undersecretary of the

Navy Ralph Bard, Adm. Lewis L. Strauss, then assistant to the secretary of the navy, and subsequently head of the Atomic Energy Commission, and President Truman himself, Teller wanted to demonstrate the power of the bomb on a noncivilian target. If, after such a demonstration, Japan did not surrender, he said, the bomb could be used without the same moral penalty.

What about President Truman's military advisors? What information and recommendations did they give the president about Japan's military capability just before he made the decision to drop the bomb?

In his war memoirs, *I Was There,* Admiral Leahy revealed that all the evidence available to him indicated that Japan was on the verge of surrender even before the bomb was dropped. In any case, he was opposed to the use of the atomic bomb on human beings both on military and moral grounds. Herewith the relevant passage from his book:

"It is my opinion that the use of this barbarous weapon at Hiroshima and Nagasaki was of no material assistance in our war against Japan. The Japanese were already defeated and ready to surrender because of the effective sea blockade and the successful bombing with conventional weapons . . . My own feeling is that in being the first to use it [the atomic bomb], we had adopted an ethical standard common to the barbarians of the Dark Ages."

Leahy also observed, "I was not taught to make war in that fashion, and wars cannot be won by destroying women and children . . ."

What advice was given to the president by Gen. George C. Marshall, chief of staff? According to a memorandum written by Assistant Secretary of War John J. McCloy, General Marshall told the president he didn't think a nuclear explosive should be used against human beings unless absolutely necessary. He therefore advised the president to have a demonstration bombing—perhaps against a naval installation distant from a population center.

Official military assessment of the decision to use the atomic bomb is provided in the U.S. Strategic Bombing Survey's 1946 publication entitled "Japan's Struggle to End the War." Even if the atomic bomb had not been dropped, the Survey found, "air supremacy over Japan could have exerted sufficient pressure to bring about unconditional surrender and obviate the need for invasion . . . certainly prior to 31 December, 1945, and in all probability prior to 1 November, 1945."

Other military estimates at the time confirmed the recognition that the war with Japan would have ended as early as September or October without the use of the bomb. Air Force Gen. Henry H. Arnold is quoted in the book, *The Armed Forces in World War II*, as saying that Japan would have had to surrender without the use of the bomb and before the proposed invasion.

In his book, *Men and Decisions*, Admiral Strauss says that "the Japanese were nearly ready to capitulate . . ." Undersecretary of the Navy Bard protested the use of the bomb without specific warning to the Japanese, even arranging a meeting with President Truman to express his concerns.

As mentioned elsewhere in this book, General MacArthur was not consulted about the decision to drop the bomb. He believed that Japan would have quit the war weeks earlier, without the use of the bomb, if the United States had agreed, as it did eventually anyway, to the request of the Japanese government that the emperor be retained. MacArthur also referred to the fact that Japan's desire to surrender was made known to the president from a number of quarters. For example, in April 1945, Allen Dulles and his associates in the Office of Strategic Services who were handling secret operations in Switzerland reported that Japanese military officials wished to make use of secret channels to "secure peace for Japan."

Meanwhile, as President Eisenhower wrote in his memoirs, once the United States had a weapon of unsurpassed power, it knew it could defeat Japan before the Soviet Union could share in the spoils of victory.

This need for haste may also explain why President Truman abandoned his intention to issue a warning about the bomb. Similarly, it may explain why Gen. George C. Marshall's recommendation for a demonstration bombing was not accepted. Finally, it may explain why a similar proposal from leading atomic scientists was rejected.

In order to create a proper perspective for the proposal of the atomic scientists, consider their report to the War Department on June 11, 1945—one month before the New Mexico test, two months before Hiroshima. The report was made by a committee on Social and Political Implications consisting of three physicists, three chemists, and one biologist under the chairmanship of Professor James Frank, of the University of Chicago. This report, not made public by the War Department at the time, is one of the most important documents of the period—even though it was virtually unknown to the American people. It was, in effect, a declaration of conscience and responsibility by scientists—a declaration that their first duty was to the general welfare, that they did not propose to stand aside in parched detachment while the products of their research were applied.

"In the past," they wrote, "scientists could disclaim direct responsibility for the use to which mankind had put their disinterested discoveries. We now feel compelled to take a more active stand because the success which we have achieved in the development of nuclear power is fraught with infinitely greater dangers than were all the inventions of the past. All of us, familiar with the present state of nucleonics, live with the vision before our eyes of sudden destruction visited on our own country, of a Pearl Harbor disaster repeated a thousand-fold magnification in every one of our major cities."

Soberly, and with great simplicity, they went on to show why no defense could be devised to offer *adequate* protection against a surprise atomic attack, and why only *adequate* international political organization of the world could offer any hope of security. They demonstrated why there were actually no "secrets" that other nations could not develop for themselves, working with the actual knowledge of nucleonics existing in scientific laboratories throughout the world, and that all we had was a head start of perhaps a few short years.

They explained the peculiar vulnerability of America to atomic attack; why our densely populated metropolitan districts and our concentrated industries could be destroyed by instant and synchronized sabotage, if not by overhead attack. They explained why a quantitative advantage in atomic bombs was only an illusory advantage. "We are in a less favorable position than nations which are either now more diffusely populated and whose industries are more scattered or whose governments have unlimited power over the movement of population and location of industrial plants . . . Russia and China are the only great nations at present which could survive a nuclear attack."

Because of all this, the report said, it was of critical importance that the bomb not be introduced in a way that would jeopardize America's long-range security, however great the apparent short-range advantages. A surprise attack by us with this new weapon—without any advance demonstration and without any ultimatum—involved much more than local military consideration. It required a political decision on the highest level. "Russia, and even allied countries which bear less mistrust of our ways and intentions, as well as neutral countries, may be deeply shocked by this step . . . It may be very difficult to persuade the world that a nation which was capable of secretly preparing and suddenly releasing a new weapon, as indiscriminate as the rocket bomb and a thousand times more destructive, is to be trusted later in any proclaimed desire of having such weapons abolished by international agreement . . . It is not at all certain that American public opinion, if it could be enlightened as to the effect of atomic explosives, would approve of our own country being the first to introduce such an indiscriminate method of wholesale destruction of civilian life.

"Thus . . . the military advantages and the saving of American lives achieved by the sudden use of atomic bombs against Japan may be outweighed by the ensuing loss of confidence and by a wave of horror and revulsion sweeping over the rest of the world."

Taking all this into account, the report recommended that the new weapon be demonstrated before the world, to be witnessed by representatives of the United Nations. The test bombing would be held on a barren island with appropriate safeguards.

What was happening was that the scientists were looking ahead and trying to establish a sound basis for international agreement with reliable safeguards.

"The best possible atmosphere for the achievement of an international agreement could be achieved if America could say to the world: 'You see what sort of weapon we had but did not use. We are ready to renounce its use in the future if other nations join us in this renunciation and agree to the establishment of an efficient international control.'

"After such a demonstration, the weapon might perhaps be used against Japan if the sanction of the United Nations (and of public opinion at home) were obtained, perhaps after a preliminary ultimatum to Japan to surrender or at least to evacuate certain regions as an alternative to their total destruction.

"This may sound fantastic, but in nuclear weapons we have something entirely new in order of magnitude of destructive power, and if we want to capitalize fully on the advantage their possession gives us, we must use new and imaginative methods."

The scientists expressed their conviction that a unilateral approach to the dropping of the atomic bomb, even apart from overwhelming moral considerations, would almost inevitably result in unilateral action by other nations. We would be undermining a possible common ground upon which common controls might later be built. As a corollary, we would be destroying whatever stand we might later decide to take on outlawing the use of atomic weapons in warfare. It would be naive to expect other nations to take such a plea seriously in view of our own lack of reticence in dropping the bomb when the war was on the very verge of being won without it.

As mentioned earlier, for a brief moment at Potsdam, President Truman himself decided, as his diary revealed, to move along these general lines—at least to the extent of issuing a warning or ultimatum to Japan. A parallel decision was that the bomb would not be used on a populous target. But these first impulses were put aside in favor of the arguments for using the bomb as a demonstration of America's power in the competition with the Soviet Union.

To summarize: President Truman's diary and the testimony of

other officials reveal that just the fact of Russian entry into the war would have been enough to bring about Japan's surrender. The main objective, therefore, was to defeat Japan *before* the Russian entry. The original intention to issue a warning or ultimatum about the bomb was shelved because of the need to meet a deadline.

This is the unvarnished picture. It was not the picture that was presented to the American people; but it illustrates the tendency of power to sweep everything aside and cause even good men to go outside the traditions of a free society in justifying their decisions. This is said not so much in judgment of the president as of the pressures of power on the presidency that tend to put short-term political needs ahead of the historical position of a society. George F. Kennan has quoted Gibbon as saying of Belisarius of Byzantium: "His imperfections flowed from the contagion of the times; his virtues were his own." Perhaps the same might be said of Harry S Truman.

Some may argue that the president was right in trying to end the war before the Russians came in. It may be considerably more difficult, however, to defend the proposition that Truman was justified in falsifying his reasons and distorting history.

It was true, as President Truman told the American people, that the atomic explosive provided the United States with the means to defeat the Japanese without an invasion. What the president did not say, however, was that his own military believed an invasion to be unnecessary because Japan's ability to fight was crumbling and that he himself believed the scheduled entry of the Soviet Union into the war would have brought about Japan's surrender.

Nor did the president tell the American people that an important factor in the decision to drop the bomb on human beings was the desire to make the Soviet Union "more manageable" in the postwar world.

The deaths, therefore, of at least 200,000 human beings at Hiroshima and Nagasaki were connected not just to the need to defeat Japan but to the president's decision to demonstrate American power as a means of strengthening our postwar posture in dealing with the Soviet Union.

As the atomic scientists had anticipated, any theoretical short-term gains achieved by the use of the bomb were more than offset by the stage that was set for an atomic armaments race and, indeed, world nuclear proliferation.

It may be argued that the use of the atomic bomb on Hiroshima and Nagasaki represented only a quantitative destructive difference from the bombings of London, Birmingham, Manchester, Berlin, Essen, Aachen, Cologne, Dusseldorf, and Tokyo itself. There comes a point, however, when differences in degree become differences in substance. The development of a device that can lead to the extermination not just of entire cities but of human society as an organized entity calls for a special understanding of its implications and consequences.

Few men understood the problems and tendencies of power better than the architects of the United States Constitution. Their reading of history taught them that good government required much more than the presence of good men in public office. Good government, as the men of the Philadelphia Constitutional Convention saw it, called for effective brakes on the exercise of power. They recognized the need for adequate authority to deal with urgent and far-reaching problems; but they were careful to surround such authority with essential restraints and constraints. Even good men, they believed, have a tendency to use whatever power they have to shield themselves from the consequences of their errors. Public scrutiny tends to be resisted, especially if it involves political penalties.

But the American Founding Fathers could not have anticipated the advent of nuclear power or the inability of policy-makers to understand its implications fully or to stay within the framework of a free society in dealing with it.

The decision of President Truman to drop atomic bombs on large aggregations of human beings may be a significant example of the way even good men can incorrectly assess and mishandle unprecedented power. It is possible that nothing that has happened since 1945 calls for more thought by the American people than that decision. It represented more than an effort to bring about a rapid end to the war with Japan; it had implications on almost everything that has happened since. It involved deep historical and philosophical issues—whether the American people are entitled to accurate information on key questions; whether a nation is morally obligated, even in war, to respect limits to unnecessary killing and devastation. Admiral Leahy's statement that he was not taught to make war in this fashion is especially relevant.

Power has a way of victimizing its users. It tends to create a dark and subterranean world in which decisions affecting the life of a nation can be taken without reference to their moral implications or the obligations to inform the people truthfully about issues of transcendent importance to their well-being and indeed survival. The power of the bomb was allowed to supersede the ultimate power of the American people.

The decision to drop the bomb on Hiroshima is a prime reflection of the idea—more than an idea, it is almost an article of faith—that the demonstration of power is a major function of foreign policy. The dangers inherent in such a policy become explosive when other nations hold to the same idea.

It is said that the Japanese can look to Pearl Harbor for the origins of the decision to drop nuclear bombs on their cities. If reprisal and retaliation are valid arguments here, the fire-bombings of Tokyo and other Japanese cities can be said to have accomplished that purpose. Hiroshima is a special case, a very special case.

3

Visit to
Hiroshima

I n 1949, I visited Hiroshima. The most startling information I encountered concerned the number of casualties. I had an opportunity to talk to Mayor Shinzo Hamai about the official figures. A cross-check had been made, I was told, comparing the body count of the dead with a population count three months after the bombing. Taking into account those who had died since the explosion, these figures showed a population decrease of 110,000. In addition, thousands of troops had been stationed on the site of the old Castle grounds near the center of the bombing; some 30,000 of these soldiers perished. In addition, thousands of volunteers from outlying areas had come to the city to help construct fire-retention barriers. When all these categories were included, the death toll was closer to 175,000 than to the 75,000 figure repeatedly used by the United States.

I asked Mayor Hamai whether the city's official figures had been made available to the United States government. It was his understanding, he said, that such had been the case. Since the American estimates were said to be based on Japanese reports, the persistent use of erroneous figures in official American estimates was puzzling, to say the least. Were we trying to minimize the damage for political reasons, especially in view of reports that the atomic bombing of Hiroshima and Nagasaki had not been necessary to end the war?

Another troubling question concerned the work of the U.S.

Atomic Bomb Casualty Commission (ABCC), which was staffed by American medical personnel. The ABCC was housed in large quarters, where thousands of survivors were examined medically but not treated. This produced the anomaly of a man suffering from radiation burns who was receiving medical analysis costing thousands of dollars but not one cent for medical treatment. The only apparent reason for this grim paradox was that we didn't want to deprive Japanese physicians of access to patients, although Japanese doctors to whom I spoke not only recognized no infringement but were disturbed by the impact of U.S. policy on the survivors. So, indeed, were many of the American doctors, who found ways of circumventing the regulations. American and Japanese physicians created informal alliances in which they cooperated in providing much-needed care. As this arrangement progressed, it did a great deal to offset the unfortunate early effects on public opinion in the city.

At the time of my visit, many of the city's wounds were still open; from my hotel window, I could see perhaps six square miles of the city, stretching along the banks of its rivers, and sprawling out beyond. The city itself is fairly flat, built on sea level. Hiroshima is a seaport, though from that vantage point it seemed completely surrounded by a ring of mountains. The hurry-up, improvised quality of the wooden buildings on the other side of the river gave the city something of the appearance of an American mining town in the West a century ago. This resemblance was even stronger because of the mountains in the background.

I could also see, from my window, the general area hit hardest by the atomic bomb; I could see what became the most famous landmark of the atomic explosion—the dome, or what used to be a dome, of the old Industrial Exhibition Hall. It was hollowed out, but just enough of the curved steelwork was left so you could tell it was a dome. Then there was another four- or five-story structure off to the left a few hundred yards away that showed evidence of considerable damage, but apart from these two buildings Hiroshima had been completely rebuilt—rebuilt, that is, on a sort of overnight basis. The homes, the stores, the industrial buildings were thrown up very hastily. But the greatest difficulty hadn't been putting up the new

buildings and shacks. The greatest difficulty had been in clearing
away the rubble.

The river was at low tide. It was possible to walk across its full
width of about 500 feet without getting your ankles wet. Across the
river, the streets were clearly marked out. There was very little open
area; you saw no rubble or evidence of the bomb whatsoever, except
for the old dome skeleton.

Of course, when you actually walked through the street you
could see many wounds. You saw the gutted foundations of the
concrete buildings, even though four years of weeds and grass did
a great deal to smooth over and conceal the old ruins. Right next
to the small inn where I stayed was the wreckage of what was once
a fairly large two-story stone home. All that was left was part of a
wall, the large concrete gateposts, and the iron gate itself—most of
it twisted out of shape. I went poking around behind the wall and
came across a family of five living under a piece of canvas, propped
up by boards, and using the stone wall as the principal inside wall
surface. Right in front of this home, if you could call it that, which
measured about seven feet by seven feet, the family had cleared away
the rubble and planted a vegetable garden.

I stood at the spot which was believed to mark the center of the
atomic explosion. Directly in front of me were two fairly thick and
round stucco columns or gateposts on a very small plot raised about
one foot off the ground level as a marker and memorial. These
columns were all that was left of a hospital, directly under the atomic
burst. A new hospital had been built right in back of the old gateposts. It was a two-story affair, painted white. Patients waved to us
from the windows.

As I stood at the center of the atomic explosion, it was difficult
to describe the things I felt. Here, only a few years earlier, there was
a flash of heat which at the split second of fission was many times
the surface temperature of the sun. And suddenly, even before a stop
watch could register it, the heart of a city was laid open with a hot
knife. I talked to dozens of people who were in it—dozens who were
crippled and burned and suffering from diseases of radioactivity—
and the story was very much the same. The sudden flash of light

brighter than the morning sun, much more intense than lightning, much more intense than any light ever seen before on this earth. If you lived through that second, you found that your clothes were on fire, and you rushed out into the street and ran, for everyone else was running—no one knew where. And everything was now blazing and you were inside the fire, trying to run somewhere. Then someone yelled, "Run for the river!" and you threw yourself into the river and thousands of others did the same thing and you wondered what happened to your family, to your children or your parents. No one knew where anyone was, but there were people all around you, and other people were jumping from the bridges into the river, and the dead bodies were all around you in the river, but you could hardly hear the people crying out because the blaze was like rolling thunder sweeping over you. And all day and night the fire ate your city and burned your dead, and all night you stayed in the river to cool your burns, but the tide ran out and you buried yourself as deeply in the mud as you could and prayed for the tide to come back in again with the water from the sea to cool your fevered body, even though it was salt water and threw knives into your burns, but at least they were cool knives. The hours passed slowly and you searched the sky for the light of morning, but the city was a torch and it was difficult to see the sky. But then morning came and you joined the thousands of others stumbling over the wreckage of the buildings, the sounds of the dying and the damned all around you. You were too much in a hurry to notice you had no clothes; it was hard to see that the others had no clothes either, for their bodies were like charcoal.

This then was Hiroshima in the first hours of the Atomic Age. It was something new in the solar system—getting at the heart of matter and ripping it apart, causing the smallest units of nature to smash each other and set off a flash as though a piece of the sun itself had broken away, and sending out strange rays that went through the bones and did things to the composition of human blood that had not been done before or dreamt of before. This was the triumph of mind over matter in the ultimate and most frightening sense.

As I stood in front of the large stone columns from the old hospital gateposts and reached over and felt the rough, raised surface of the stone, its composition altered because the surface had been melted by the explosion, I wondered why people would ever come back to the city again—not merely Hiroshima but any city—any city that man ever built, for by this bomb he had placed a curse on every city everywhere. I wondered what the lure could be that could bring people out from the hills and back to this place of compressed agony. I wondered but I didn't have very far to look for the answer, for the answer was all around me. I could see it in the faces of the people who passed on the street. I could see it in the brisk, life-loving walk of the young people. I could hear it in the full laughter of children. I could see it in the eagerness of young boys and young men playing ball with each other wherever there was a place to play ball. The answer I found was that there are deeper resources of courage and regeneration in human beings than any of the philosophers had dared to dream. The greatest force on earth—greater than any war device or explosive—is the will to live and the capacity for hope. As I looked around, I saw a young woman with a baby strapped to her back. She was wearing Western dress though she had on Japanese wooden shoes. There was nothing defeatist about this woman. She was starting out to raise a family; she was going to do it in Hiroshima, and nowhere else; she believed in life, and nothing could change it. And as she passed, I looked at the back of her neck and down her left arm, and saw the seared and discolored flesh that was the badge of citizenship in Hiroshima. The woman stepped to one side to allow a modern bus to pass—it was a bus filled with Japanese baseball players in uniform, for baseball had become the national pastime in Japan to an extent not approached even in America. The baseball players were singing, some of them, and I thought I saw, but I couldn't be quite sure, the familiar atomic burns on one or two arms or faces.

Another thing I wondered about was what the people themselves thought about the bomb and about America. I spoke to them about it, and it was hard to believe that what they said was the way people can or should feel after having lived through an atomic explosion. There was no bitterness, except in one or two cases. They said, most of them, that if it hadn't been Hiroshima it would have been another city and they had no right to ask exemption at the expense of their fellows. They said, most of them, that they had taken part in something that would save the lives of millions, for they believed, most of them, that Hiroshima, in the words of Mayor Hamai, was an exhibit for peace, a laboratory that had demonstrated the nature of the new warfare so dramatically that it would destroy war itself. Some of them, of course, said things they thought I wanted to hear, but their voices and their eyes would frequently give them away. And then, as counterbalance perhaps, I would find a woman—a woman barber who had lost her husband and two children in the bombing—and she couldn't understand why such a fiendish weapon was necessary against civilians. Then there were some who blamed it on the Japanese government; they said that when Japan first bombed China they were certain that God would visit the crime on the Japanese a thousandfold. Some blamed it on the Japanese government because it had converted Hiroshima into a military base and shipping point, and they were certain that America would find this out and destroy the city.

This was the first I had heard about Hiroshima as a city of military importance. As I spoke to people and questioned them, the picture began to take shape. When a girl of nineteen told me about her experience in the bombing, she spoke of all the soldiers running past her house on the way from the barracks near the old Castle. When the photographer who took films for me told about his experience during the bombing, he spoke of his sensation while riding a train two miles away from Hiroshima on his way to work. He said that when he heard the explosion he thought the large ammunition supply center near the old Parade Grounds had been blown up, for the explosion was too loud for even the largest bomb. Others on the outskirts of the city spoke of the same feeling. I spoke to one man who operated a bus to the ammunition dump; he gave me some idea of its size and said that many thousands worked there during the war.

It was freely admitted, once I referred to it, that Japan was divided into two main military zones, and that the headquarters for the North was in Tokyo, and the headquarters for the South in Hiroshima.

Later that evening I discussed with Mayor Hamai the military importance of Hiroshima during the war. He spoke freely and fully. Hiroshima had been Japan's chief port for sending soldiers overseas. It had housed large ammunition supply depots.

I asked the mayor whether it was true, as I had heard in some of my conversations, that as many as 60,000 soldiers had been stationed in Hiroshima at the time of the bombing. He was familiar with the reports but believed that the number may have been closer to 40,000. Then I learned for the first time that this figure had been suppressed by the Japanese police, then under orders from the Japanese government to conceal the military death toll and the military importance of Hiroshima as well as to minimize the general damage and civilian death toll. Japan had been taken completely by surprise and didn't want the United States to know how effective the weapon had been, so that what little bargaining power she had at the peace table might not have been further reduced.

The following day, Mayor Hamai took me on a tour of Hiroshima's hospitals. It was an experience difficult to put out of my mind. I saw things that hammered at my sanity. I saw beds held together with slabs of wood; nowhere did I see sheets or pillows. I saw dirty bandages and littered floors; I saw rooms not much larger than closets with four or five patients huddled together. I thought back to what I had seen in the displaced persons camps in Germany and I knew that nothing I had seen in Germany or anywhere else put human pride to such a strain.

I looked in on an operating room that seemed little better than a crude abattoir. I saw rooms where whole families had moved in with the patient. I saw all this with unbelieving eyes and then had some idea of what Mayor Hamai meant when he said that Hiroshima needed America's help to take care of its sick. All the hospitals in Hiroshima were destroyed or gutted or severely damaged by the bomb, and hospital facilities in Japan were not easy to come by. People can throw up shacks as homes inside a week or two, but a hospital is nothing to be thrown together. There was need of surgical equipment and rubber gloves for operations and sterilizers and X-ray equipment and beds and pots and pans.

On the second floor of the Memorial Hospital in Hiroshima, near crowded rooms of children who were serious TB cases, a woman rushed out to me and fell at my feet, sobbing. Dr. Akio Asano, the tall, scholarly, youthful head of the hospital, told me the woman had heard that an American had come to Hiroshima and that she had just been praying to Kami for the American to come to the hospital so that he might be able to see how sick her little girl was and how badly she needed certain medicine they didn't have in Hiroshima. She was still praying when I walked in. The little girl was seven years old. Her father had been killed in the atomic explosion. Her name was Nobuko Takeuchi. She had been ill from tuberculosis for several months, complicated by a series of mastoid infections, for which there had been several operations. But now she had what Dr. Asano described as the worst case of tuberculosis he had ever seen in a child of her age, and she might not live for more than a few weeks unless she was able to get large doses of streptomycin. But nowhere in Hiroshima could you get streptomycin.

That night I became a black marketeer. I established contact with what are called sources in Japan and a few grams of streptomycin were rushed over to the hospital. But little Nobuko needed forty to fifty grams and we sent wires to Tokyo and even to the United States to get the medicine in time. Three days after my first visit to Dr. Asano's hospital Nobuko was still getting along on the first few grams. In response to the wires, a considerable supply of streptomycin was sent by the Church World Service. It arrived in Hiroshima by air several days later, and Dr. Asano reported that Nobuko had responded to the medicine.

After we left the hospital, Mayor Hamai told me of his dream for a modern hospital in Hiroshima that would become part of the Hiroshima Peace Center, for which the Rev. Kiyoshi Tanimoto, of the Nakaregawa Church of Christ in Hiroshima, had gone to the United States in search of support. I had been working with Mr. Tanimoto in the United States, getting groups together to advance the idea of a Hiroshima Peace Center, but not until then did I realize how important were the units that were to go into it. The Peace Center would have, in addition to the hospital, an orphanage, a home for the aged, a civic recreation center, a peace institute study center, and a medical research center.

The next tour was of the orphanages for children whose parents were killed in the atomic explosion. One of them in particular—the Yamashita Orphanage, located about eight miles outside the city on a hillside—was operated by Mr. and Mrs. Yamashita as a public service with whatever help and support they could get from the city and its people, and from the outside world. It was the largest of the four orphanages for Hiroshima children, providing care for almost 100 youngsters ranging in age from four years to seventeen years. The youngest was born just a few hours before the bombing.

Mr. and Mrs. Yamashita were able to survive the bombing despite severe burns. Mrs. Yamashita had been close to the center of the explosion and said that suddenly there was a bright light and her body was on fire. She was carrying her two-year-old baby at the time, and the first thing she did was to smother the flames that enveloped the child. Then she picked up the baby and ran until she reached the fields outside the city, where she lived for three days on the ground before word came that people were returning to the city.

On her return she found Mr. Yamashita already under treatment. Recovery was slow for both of them, but after six months they were able to resume their lives and decided to dedicate themselves to the care of orphans. They acquired land and homes outside Hiroshima and built the little colony.

Mr. and Mrs. Yamashita were completely recovered by 1949, except that the old wounds burned and itched in extremely warm or cold weather. Mrs. Yamashita said that she had been unable to have a successful pregnancy since the bombing, having experienced four miscarriages. She spoke of other women in Hiroshima in like circumstances.

The Yamashita Orphanage was, I think, the high spot of my visit to Hiroshima. Living conditions were better and brighter than I had seen almost anywhere else in the city. The children there were more alert, more responsive, and seemed quicker and happier than I had seen almost anywhere in Japan. The food was adequate and well prepared; there was ample play space; and, what was more important, the children were not starved for want of affection. Dozens of the younger ones hung on to Mrs. Yamashita like kids hanging on to an American mother's skirts in a department store. The quality of the teaching in the orphanage was as high as you would find anywhere in Japan. There was only one thing wrong with the Yamashita Orphanage. There was not enough of it. It should have been five times as large.

Before coming to Japan, several people had told me that they would like to adopt Japanese children orphaned by the bombing. Under the Oriental Exclusion Act, however, these adoptions were not possible. I suggested the next best thing—moral adoptions. By moral adoptions I was thinking of Hiroshima children who would be adopted by American families and who would carry the names of the people adopting them. The children would continue to live in Japan—perhaps in some place such as Mrs. Yamashita's—but the American families would be responsible for their care and upbringing. Then, later, if Congress passed a law permitting Japanese children to come to America, these morally adopted children could become legally adopted as well.

The full cost of taking care of one child at Mrs. Yamashita's—including food, education, and everything else—was $2.25 a month! I proposed the idea of moral adoptions to Mrs. Yamashita and she was enthusiastic about it.

The next morning, Mayor Hamai took me to the site of the old Castle that had been destroyed by the bomb. Here, on an artificial hillside, I could overlook the city with its seven rivers and its many bridges. I could see the many homes and stores going up. The sound of the city, with its old trolleys, and the sounds of the pile drivers and the hammers and saws, blended into a drone, as it sometimes does high up in a skyscraper.

There on the hillside that morning, a small group of citizens broke ground for the Hiroshima Peace Center, and rededicated their city to the cause of peace by renaming it the Peace City. Mayor

Hamai spoke of his hope that within a few years there might rise on this site an Institute for the Study of World Peace, as part of the Peace Center project.

The day before I left Hiroshima, I asked Mayor Hamai whether there was anything he wanted me to do for him in the United States. He hesitated a while, then said he would like me to bring back a message from him to Americans. He wrote it out:

There is much I would like to say to America. First of all, I would like to thank those Americans who have helped us to bring a dead city back to life.

It is not my place or purpose to try to tell Americans what ought to be done. But what I can do is to tell them about what will happen to the world's cities if something is not done to stop war. The people of Hiroshima ask nothing of the world except that we be allowed to offer ourselves as an exhibit for peace. We ask only that enough people know what happened here and how it happened and why it happened, and that they work hard to see that it never happens anywhere again.

We the people of Hiroshima are sick at heart as we look out at the world and see that nations are already fighting the initial skirmishes that can grow into a full war. We know that stopping war is not a simple thing and that there are grave questions that have to be solved before the world can have true peace. We know, too, that peace is not to be had just for the asking; all nations must agree to it.

But we also know that some nation must take leadership in building the type of peace that will last. And we are looking to America for that leadership . . . the world will listen. Leaders of a few nations may not want to listen but their people will hear. This is the best hope for averting a war which would see thousands of Hiroshimas. And this is the message the people of Hiroshima ask that you take back to America.

4

General MacArthur
in Fact
and Fiction

ouglas MacArthur is one of the most heralded military heroes in American history. His name is most closely associated with America's comeback in power and prestige after the disaster of Pearl Harbor at the outset of World War II. But MacArthur is also one of the most complex and enigmatic figures in the twentieth century. To some Americans, he was the supreme symbol of our undefeated record in war; they saw him as fearless, uncompromising, victory-minded. To other Americans, he seemed to represent a man on a white horse riding to power at the expense of democratic institutions.

But the real MacArthur didn't quite conform to the view of him held by either his admirers or his detractors. He was not a lover of big bombs or a brandisher of hot swords. He was not fitted to a white horse or to any of the extremist platforms from which a strong man would pronounce and denounce, propose and dispose. Yes, there was grandeur to the man. He could be hard, haughty, impatient. He could drive forward when he had an objective to reach, and he was disdainful of obstructions. And no one surpassed his genius for invoking patriotism. But he was not a tub-thumping jingoist who contrived to juxtapose the national cause against the human cause. He may have been autocratic in manner but he was democratic in purpose. His main job in life was done in soldier's uniform but this was not the way he wanted ultimately to be remembered.

"Could I have but a line a century hence crediting a contribution to the advance of peace," he once said, "I would gladly yield every honor which has been accorded me in war."

And again, he had expressed the hope that if a future historian should judge him worthy "of some slight reference," it would be not as a military commander but as a man determined to create a genuine basis for justice and peace.

In the headlines and newspaper stories after his death, what he had prayed would not happen did happen. They extolled him as a great military figure, which he was, but they gave very little notice to the things of which he was proudest and which may have helped to change history for the better. He was proud to be called the liberator of the Philippines but he was at least equally proud of his insistence that the civilian government of the Philippines come ahead of the military. He was proud to have received the articles of military surrender from the Japanese, but he was even prouder that the central purpose of his occupation was to create civilian rule within the shortest possible time. And he was especially proud that Japan was the first nation in human history to renounce war and the means of war.

This renunciation was written into the new Japanese Constitution that took shape under the Occupation. Two other features of that constitution he believed were also of historic significance. One was the clause decreeing the end of feudalism and the social injustices inherent in it. The second was a bill of rights and the establishment of an independent judiciary.

He regarded the Japanese Constitution not merely as an expression of ultimate aspiration but as a statement of working principles. He didn't go to Japan for the purpose of helping to lay down a superficial veneer but to participate in the making of a profound revolution in the democratization of a nation—and he never hesitated to use the word "democracy" even though the extremists at home who professed to worship him had tended to shun the term. He fought against the usury that impoverished countless numbers of farmers and tradesmen. He helped to set free the largest politically and socially disenfranchised group in Japan—women. He made it possible for Japanese laborers to be represented through organized collective bargaining. He sponsored a program of land reform under which millions of acres were turned over to the peasants who had worked the land for absentee owners. The land reform program had its sanction, if not its origin, in Thomas Jefferson's agrarian philosophy. As a matter of precise historical record, the main architect of land reform in Japan was Wolf Ladejinski, a member of MacArthur's staff; but Ladejinski not only encountered no resistance but was spurred on by MacArthur, who recognized the value of that social program for Japan. Considering the fact that the redistribution of land for social purposes had been denounced at other places and in other times as a communistic scheme, MacArthur's identification with land reform was a clear indication that he was not playing to a conservative gallery.

All these were substantial achievements, and they were all interrelated; but it is possible that the clause in the Japanese Constitution renouncing war was the achievement that meant the most to him personally.

He liked to recall the time that Prime Minister Shidehara agreed with him that the best way of serving and saving Japan was by abolishing war as an international instrument. "The world will laugh at us as impractical visionaries," the prime minister said, "but a hundred years from now we will be called prophets."

MacArthur was never called a visionary; yet he felt most at home with visions of a better world.

"Many will say, with mockery and ridicule," he declared, "that the abolition of war can be only a dream—that it is but the vague imagining of a visionary. But we must go on or we will go under. And the great criticism that can be made is that the world lacks a plan that will enable us to go on."

His main rebuke of leaders in government was not so much that they interfered with the military but that they weren't sufficiently imaginative in creating the design for a world under law.

"Leaders must not be laggards," he said. "They have not even approached the basic problem, much less evolved a working formula to implement this public demand. They debate and turmoil over a hundred issues; they bring us to the verge of despair or raise our hopes to utopian heights over the corollary misunderstandings that stem from the threat of war . . . Never do they dare to state the bald truth, that the next great advance in the evolution of civilization cannot take place until war is abolished."

I had an opportunity to get to know Douglas MacArthur during the period of the American occupation of Japan, of which he was head. He was both military commander and political chief. I went to Japan at his invitation as a consultant on the broad range of problems associated with the democratization of Japan; more particularly, the area of human rights. I had several meetings with the General, apart from separate sessions with key members of his staff. Our discussions covered a wide range of subjects, including the decision to drop atomic bombs on Hiroshima and Nagasaki, and the prospects of peace in the postwar world.

MacArthur correctly anticipated that the antagonisms between the United States and the Soviet Union in the post-war world would result in American pressure on Japan to re-arm. Since he was the principal architect of the clause in the new Japanese Constitution outlawing the re-militarization of the nation, he was deeply troubled by the possibility of reversal.

Japanese militarism, he said, had been one of the prime dangers to free peoples in the twentieth century. It was only by the narrowest of margins that Japan's domination of the Pacific area and the entire Far East was averted. Countervailing democratic forces in Japan needed to be developed, nurtured, strengthened. MacArthur had committed himself to that purpose—not just as an extemporaneous response to American victory over Japan but as a deep commitment to a peaceful future. Nothing could be more shortsighted, he asserted, than to rearm Japan with the intention of shifting the balance of power in the Far East against the Soviet Union.

In the first place, it was by no means certain that the combination of militarism and the restoration of nationalism would make Japan an automatic ally of the United States in the competition between the U.S. and the USSR In the second place, a re-militarized Japan might create even greater problems for the United States than the challenges represented by Eastern Europe.

When I asked General MacArthur whether an unarmed Japan would represent a temptation to aggressor nations, he puffed thoughtfully on his pipe and said that he found it difficult to believe that Japan could achieve security by re-arming. In a world with atomic explosives, he doubted that a re-armed Japan would be anything more than a target for atomic attack. Basically, the only security he saw for Japan—or any other nation, for that matter—was through a reorganized world under the rule of law. He said that the advent of nuclear weapons had completely outmoded the traditional forms of security and sovereignty. He felt that the principal danger not just to America but to all the world's peoples stemmed from the failure to realize that military security, as the world had known it in the past, was no longer possible. What was absolutely necessary, he continued, was the need to jump far ahead in our thinking about war and peace. He believed that institutions of world law had to be developed. He saw no prospect that the heads of nations would move in this direction unless prodded by a powerful and resolute world opinion.

He said he was not impressed with arguments that the Soviet Union was an unmovable obstacle to workable world organization. The ideological struggle in the world had to give way to the requirements of mutual survival.

In stating these opinions, he foreshadowed what was probably the most important public statement of his long career. In a talk before the American Legion in Los Angeles on January 26, 1955, he outlined his thoughts about world peace. Not much news attention was given to this speech, but many of his supporters who heard it were probably surprised by his assertions about the unworkability of national sovereignty in the modern world, about the inadequacy of military supremacy, even if it could be achieved, and about the need for a worldwide public clamor to compel governments to move in the direction of an integrated world society.

It is difficult for me to think of a more appropriate or relevant statement—one that has lost none of its timeliness or force—than that 1955 speech. Such being the case, I quote from it here at length:

At the turn of the century, when I entered the Army, the target was one enemy casualty at the end of a rifle or bayonet or sword. Then came the machine gun designed to kill by the dozen. After that, the heavy artillery raining death upon the hundreds. Then the aerial bomb to strike by the thousands—followed by the atom explosion to reach the hundreds of thousands. Now, electronics and other processes of science have raised the destructive potential to encompass millions. And with restless hands we work feverishly in dark laboratories to find the means to destroy all at one blow.

But this very triumph of scientific annihilation—this very success of invention—has destroyed the possibility of war being a medium of *practical* settlement of international differences. The enormous destruction to both sides of closely matched opponents makes it impossible for the winner to translate it into anything but his own disaster.

The Second World War, even with its now antiquated armaments, clearly demonstrated that the victor had to bear in large part the very injuries inflicted on his foe. Our own country spent billions of dollars and untold energies to heal the wounds of Germany and Japan. War has become a Frankenstein to destroy both sides. No longer is it the weapon of adventure whereby a short cut to international power and wealth—a place in the sun—can be gained. If you lose, you are annihilated. If you win, you stand only to lose. No longer does it possess the chance of the winner of a duel—it contains rather the germs of double suicide. Science has clearly outmoded it as a feasible arbiter. The great question is: can war be outlawed? If so, it would mark the greatest advance in civilization since the Sermon on the Mount. It would lift at one stroke the darkest shadow which has engulfed mankind from the beginning. It would not only remove fear and bring security—it would not only create new moral and spiritual values—it would produce an economic wave of prosperity that would raise the world's standard of living beyond anything ever dreamed of by man. The hundreds of billions of dollars now spent in mutual preparedness could conceivably abolish poverty from the face of the globe. It would accomplish even more than this; it would at one stroke reduce the international tensions that seem so insurmountable now to matters of more probable solution . . .

You will say at once that although the abolition of war has been the dream of man for centuries, every proposition to that end has been promptly discarded as impossible and fantastic. Every cynic, every pessimist, every adventurer, every swashbuckler in the world has always disclaimed its feasibility. But that was before the science of the past decade made mass destruction a reality. The argument then was along spiritual and moral lines, and lost. It is a sad truth that human character has never reached a theological development which would permit the application of pure idealism. In the last two thousand years its rate of change has been deplorably slow compared to that of the arts and the sciences. But now the tremendous and present evolution of nuclear and other potentials of destruction has suddenly taken the problem away from its primary consideration as a moral and spiritual question and brought it abreast of scientific realism. It is no longer an ethical equation to be pondered solely by learned philosophers and ecclesiastics but a hard core one for the decision of the masses whose survival is the issue. This is as true of the Soviet side of the world as of the free side—as true behind the Iron Curtain as in front of it. The ordinary people of the world, whether free or slave, are all in agreement on this solution; and this perhaps is the only thing in the world they do agree upon. But it is the most vital and determinate of all. The leaders are the laggards. The disease of power seems to confuse and befuddle them. They have not even approached the basic problem, much less evolved a working formula to implement this public demand. They debate and turmoil over a hundred issues—they bring us to the verge of despair or raise our hopes to utopian heights over the corollary misunderstandings that stem from the threat of war—but never in the chancelleries of the world or the halls of the United Nations is the real problem raised. Never do they dare to state the bald truth, that the next great advance in the evolution of civilization cannot take place until war is abolished. It may take another cataclysm of destruction to prove to them this simple truth. But, strange as it may seem, it is known now by all common men. It is the one issue upon which both sides can agree, for it is the one issue upon which both sides will profit equally. It is the one issue—and the only decisive one—in which the interests of both are completely parallel. It is the one issue which, if settled, might settle all others.

Time has shown that agreements between modern nations are generally no longer honored as valid unless both profit therefrom. But both sides can be trusted when both do profit. It becomes then no longer a problem based upon relative integrity. It is now no longer convincing to argue, whether true or not, that we cannot trust the other side—that one maverick can destroy the herd. It would no longer be a matter depending upon trust—the self-interest of each nation outlawing war would keep it true to itself. And there is no influence so potent and powerful as self-interest. It would not necessarily require international inspection of relative armaments—the public opinion of every part of the world would be the great denominator which would ensure the issue—each nation would so profit that it could not fail eventually to comply. This would not, of course, mean the abandonment of all armed forces, but it would reduce them to the simpler problems of internal order and international police. It would not mean Utopia at one fell stroke, but it would mean that the great road block now existing to the development of the human race would have been cleared.

The present tensions with their threat of national annihilation are kept alive by two great illusions. The one, a complete belief on the part of the Soviet world that the capitalist countries are preparing to attack them; that sooner or later we intend to strike. And the other, a complete belief on the part of the capitalistic countries that the Soviets are preparing to attack us; that sooner or later they intend to strike. Both are wrong. Each side, so far as the masses are concerned, is equally desirous of peace. For either side, war with the other would mean nothing but disaster. Both equally dread it. But the constant acceleration of preparation may well, without specific intent, ultimately produce a spontaneous combustion.

We are told we must go on indefinitely as at present—some say fifty years or more. With what at the end? None say—there is no definite objective. They but pass along to those that follow the search for a final solution. And, at the end, the problem will be exactly the same as that which we face now. Must we live for generations under the killing punishment of accelerating preparedness without an announced final purpose or, as an alternative, suicidal war; and trifle in the meanwhile with corollary and indeterminate theses—such as limitation of armament, restriction on the use of nuclear power, adoption of new legal standards as propounded at Nuremberg—all of which are but palliatives and all of which in varying forms have been tried in the past with negligible results?

. . . Must we fight again before we learn? When will some great figure in power have sufficient imagination and moral courage to translate this universal wish—which is rapidly becoming a universal necessity—into actuality? We are in a new era. The old methods and solutions no longer suffice. We must have new thoughts, new ideas, new concepts, just as did our venerated forefathers when they faced a New World. We must break out of the strait-jacket of the past.

There must always be one to lead, and we should be that one. We should now proclaim our readiness to abolish war in concert with the great powers of the world. The result would be magical.

Douglas MacArthur is frequently juxtaposed against Dwight D. Eisenhower, much in the way that Hamilton has been contrasted with Jefferson. But MacArthur's Los Angeles speech in January 1955 was remarkably similar to Dwight Eisenhower's talk before the American Society of Newspaper Editors in April 1953, the emphasis in both speeches being on the need to look beyond military force to world institutions for genuine security. Similarly, Eisenhower's 1961 Farewell Address, made famous for its reference to the "military-industrial complex," seemed to come off the same spool as a MacArthur speech made to the Michigan State Legislature on May 15, 1952, when he cautioned America about the tendencies of the arms manufacturers to promote their own interests at the public expense. "It is part of the general pattern of misguided policy," he said, "that our country is now geared to an arms industry which was bred in an artificially induced psychosis of war hysteria and nurtured upon an incessant propaganda of fear."

These beliefs do not conform to the popular impression of MacArthur, but they represent the ultimate product of his experiences and thoughts, affected profoundly by the development of atomic weapons. The great irony of MacArthur is that he was regarded as one of America's greatest war heroes but he came to recognize that the future of the human species depended on workable alternatives to force.

MacArthur's views about the decision to drop the atomic bomb on Hiroshima and Nagasaki were starkly different from what the general public supposed. The public impression was that President Truman had decided to use the atomic bomb on the urgent advice of his military advisers. Specifically, since the bomb was used against Japan, it was widely assumed that General MacArthur, as commander of America's Far Eastern forces, was a prime factor in that advice.

When I asked General MacArthur about the decision to drop the bomb, I was surprised to learn he had not even been consulted. What, I asked, would his advice have been? He replied that he saw no military justification for the dropping of the bomb. The war might have ended weeks earlier, he said, if the United States had agreed, as it later did anyway, to the retention of the institution of the emperor.

When I asked what he had done in his long career that gave him the greatest pride, he repeated his earlier statement about the new Japanese Constitution, with its clause not just renouncing war as an instrument of national policy but the armaments with which to fight it. His final commitment was to a world without war. He said that if he were starting all over again, he felt he could best serve the American people by trying to demonstrate that the national security could no longer be adequately served by superior weapons or military force but by the abolition of war itself. Such persuasion was necessary because he didn't believe the political leaders were capable of moving, unprodded, in this direction. Whatever General MacArthur's differences may have been with General Eisenhower, they had virtually identical views about the vital role of public opinion in creating a path for peace.

It is not difficult to agree with President Truman's decision to relieve General MacArthur of his command during the Korean War in 1951. The president, under our Constitutional system, is the commander-in-chief. Whatever MacArthur's convictions about how the Korean War was to be fought, on which he had the right and indeed the obligation to press his views with the president, he did not have the right to oppose the orders of the president.

It would be a serious mistake, however, to dismiss Douglas MacArthur as a militarist who believed only in superior force. He knew that the science of destruction had made war obsolete as an instrument of national policy and that new institutions had to be developed not only to resolve disputes but to forestall or protect against aggression.

What happened on August 6, 1945, General MacArthur wrote,

was a "warning to all men of all races that the harnessing of nature's forces in furtherance of war's destructiveness will progress until the means are at hand to exterminate the human race and destroy the material structure of the modern world. This is the lesson of Hiroshima. God grant that it not be ignored."

5

Prophetic Legacy: Eisenhower's Emphasis on "True" Security

Dwight D. Eisenhower was elected to the White House on the basis of his vast popularity as an American military leader in World War II. But the years of his presidency—1953–1961—viewed in retrospect may be seen as a period of reconciliation in foreign affairs and strengthening of basic internal institutions. And the primary assessment of Eisenhower's place in American history may rest on the prophetic accuracy of his warning about the growing influence of the military and the armaments industry.

Eisenhower's reference to this danger in his Farewell Address to the American people on January 17, 1961, has given rise to two popular misconceptions. The first is that he was referring *solely* to a "military-industrial complex." The second is that his comment reflected views arrived at only late in his presidency.

The first misconception is readily dealt with, for Eisenhower also specifically referred to the "scientific-technological elite," as the following passages from the talk make clear:

In the councils of government, we must guard against the acquisition of unwarranted influence, whether sought or unsought, by the military-industrial complex. The potential for the disastrous rise of misplaced power exists and will persist. We must never let the weight of this combination endanger our liberties or democratic processes. We should take nothing for granted. Only an alert and knowledgeable citizenry can compel the proper meshing of the huge industrial and military machinery of defense with our peaceful methods and goals, so that security and liberty may prosper together.

Today, the solitary inventor, tinkering in his shop, has been overshadowed by task forces of scientists in laboratories and testing fields. In the same fashion, the free university, historically the fountainhead of free ideas and scientific discovery, has experienced a revolution in the conduct of research. Partly because of the huge costs involved, a government contract becomes virtually a substitute for intellectual curiosity. For every old blackboard there are now hundreds of new electronic computers.

The prospect of domination of the nation's scholars by Federal employment, project allocations, and the power of money is ever present—and is gravely to be regarded.

Yet, in holding scientific research and discovery in respect, as we should, we must also be alert to the equal and opposite danger that public policy could itself become the captive of a scientific-technological elite.

The second misconception—that Eisenhower's deep concern about military influence in government was arrived at only at the end of his presidency—calls for personal testimony. I write here on the basis of direct conversations with General Eisenhower—before, during, and after his presidency. In 1951, while head of NATO, he wrote me about a *Saturday Review* editorial. General Eisenhower said that he strongly agreed that the United States should embrace the concept of world law as the unifying principle of its foreign policy, but he hoped we would also recognize the need for adequate military strength until world order under law was achieved.

The ensuing correspondence led to a personal relationship that deepened after General Eisenhower returned from NATO. In July 1959, at his suggestion, I proposed to the Praesidium of the Soviet Peace Committee in Moscow a continuing series of meetings between leaders from the private sector of each country for the purpose of exploring outstanding issues between the two nations. Eisenhower believed that diplomatic negotiations sometimes bog down because each side fears a conciliatory attitude would be regarded as weakness by the other side. Private discussions, however, could probe for openings without penalty or risk to either government, enabling the diplomats to begin their talks at an advanced stage. His judgment in this respect has since been confirmed by twenty-six years of meetings between citizen leaders of both countries in what has come to be known as the Dartmouth Conference series. (The first meeting was held at Dartmouth College Hanover, New Hampshire.)

The Dartmouth Conferences have played an exploratory and helpful role in bringing about the end of atmospheric testing, the development of cultural exchanges, direct air connections, the hot line, widening of trade, and arms-control talks.

In September 1960, only a few months before the end of his term of office, I had an opportunity to talk with the president at the New York Waldorf-Astoria apartment of the U.S. Ambassador to the UN President Eisenhower had come to New York for an appearance at the United Nations General Assembly. His mood was confident, upbeat. In fact, I hadn't remembered seeing him in such fine form since he came to office—and I said something to that effect.

The president grinned and said the appearance probably reflected the reality. He was full of anticipations, saying he looked forward to leaving the presidency so that he could devote himself to the cause of world peace.

I suppose my jaw dropped open at the implications of the remark. I think he enjoyed the effect of his quixotic statement, for he smiled and said he relished the notion of being able to speak out as a citizen, free of the gauntlets that even a president has to run in the formation of foreign policy. He then referred to the multiplicity of presences and pressures inside the government. The president, he said, has the Constitutional responsibility for shaping foreign policy. The Department of State is the prescribed vehicle for carrying out that policy. However, as matters evolved over the years—especially since World War II—the making of foreign policy had become increasingly diffused. An "inner State Department" grew up within the White House staff, with separate "desks" corresponding to different areas of the world, and with its own intelligence operations. Added to this was the fact that the Department of Defense had its own "assessments" capability, with units throughout the world, pressing its own foreign policy recommendations on the president.

Yet another reference point in the conduct of U.S. foreign policy, of course, was the CIA Established by the Congress as an intelligence agency, the CIA became a center for clandestine operations, working with unvouchered funds and involving the United States in military operations, often without the knowledge of the American press or public. Not infrequently, the effect of CIA action had been to limit the options of the president by confronting the White House with actions from which the president could not readily withdraw.

To be sure, the president pointed out, most of these diverse influences or pressures came together in the National Security Council, but it was not unusual for the particularized views of each unit to be urged on the president away from meetings of the council. In addition, the president was under pressure from the special committees of Congress, with the Senate and House not always agreeing between themselves. What this all meant was that the conduct of U.S. policy required extraordinary skills in the balancing of competing pressures.

I asked the president about the U-2 episode. The U.S. spy plane had been shot down over the Soviet Union on May 1, 1960, just as final arrangements were being made for a summit meeting with Premier Khrushchev scheduled for May 16 in Paris. In the crossfire of public pronouncements and alarming headlines that followed the downing of the plane, prospects for the summit appeared shaky, but neither side backed off. On May 14, President Eisenhower and his party went to Paris. The initial meeting among Eisenhower, Khrushchev, Macmillan, and De Gaulle, on May 16, had scarcely begun when Khrushchev jumped to his feet and launched into a tirade, demanding an apology from Eisenhower. The president refused, saying that he had come to Paris in anticipation of serious discussions and hoped the meeting could continue on substantive issues, at which point Khrushchev and the Russian delegation stalked out of the room, ending the meeting.

Eisenhower had insisted on personally approving every U-2 flight and had repeatedly expressed his reluctance about the program to the senior officials involved. He had questioned the wisdom of a flight so close to the time of the summit meeting but had been assured that the flights were too high for Soviet missiles, and that, in any case, the pilots were provided with means to destroy the planes and to commit suicide if necessary. As a result of the aborted Paris meeting, relations between the two countries suffered a major setback just at a moment when a new form of détente appeared likely.

The president said that few events in his career troubled him more deeply. He had been looking forward to the face-to-face meeting with Premier Khrushchev. He had a fair degree of confidence that it would have been possible to come to workable agreements in the interests of both countries. Bringing the arms race under control had been at the top of the agenda. He was convinced that, whatever the underlying ideological difficulties between the two countries, putting an end to the volatile and insane competition in weaponry was of vital importance. No, he said, he was not pleased by the outcome of the U-2 episode. Nor was he unaware that some people in government—whether in the State Department or the Pentagon or even in the White House—were relieved when the meeting was aborted. Direct exchanges between the president and the Soviet leader were not matters over which the State Department was especially enthusiastic.

The appointment of John Foster Dulles as secretary of state early in Eisenhower's administration might have been expected to relieve the president of many of these multiple pressures, but it also produced a considerable amount of frustration and exasperation. There was a stark difference of style and thrust between the two men. Eisenhower favored the open, direct approach. He wanted face-to-face meetings, especially with the Soviet leaders. Dulles liked to play it close to the vest. Eisenhower advocated, within the government, the broadest possible sharing of information with the American public. Not only did he not fear public opinion; he saw it as a resource. Dulles, however, regarded public opinion as an encumbrance rather than a natural ally. He tended to mix theology and ideology, with strongly held views about the integrated and monolithic nature of world communism, views which were to disadvantage the United States in dealing with the breakaway forces inside

Central Europe, or in assessing the later confrontations between the Soviet Union and the People's Republic of China over territorial and national issues, and in coping with the situation in Indo-China after the departure of the French.

One incident served to epitomize the president's personal feelings about Dulles. He told me the story of his heart attack in 1955. The pressures of the White House had been particularly heavy and his doctors had been urging him to break away. But the hoped-for respite had to be deferred week after week. Finally, an opportunity for a long weekend presented itself and he took off for Denver, for a few days of clear air and open sky.

On the first day, the president started out on his round of golf but it took him three holes before he was able to shake himself loose from trailing Washington preoccupations. On the fourth tee, however, he felt himself relaxing, and he began to relish the verdant surroundings and the clear air. Just as he was addressing the ball, however, a golf cart drove up and the driver said that an official and urgent telephone call had just come in from the White House.

The president jumped into the cart and was driven to the clubhouse. The telephone operator said the party at the other end had disconnected. The president checked with several White House aides. None of them knew anything about an "urgent" call. Out of sorts, the president drove back to the fourth tee. He resumed the game but felt uneasy. What was the telephone call all about? How was it that no one at the White House knew about it?

It took about three more holes before he was able to get back into the flow of the game. At just about that time, however, the messenger drove up again. The official and urgent telephone call was now ready.

When the president picked up the phone at the clubhouse, the caller identified himself as an aide to Secretary Dulles. Something had come up in connection with the Middle East and it was felt that the president's advice was required. The president listened very carefully and realized that the situation could not even vaguely be classified as an emergency. Why, then, he asked, did the aide not consult Secretary Dulles? The aide said that the secretary was away on a brief holiday and left instructions that he was not to be disturbed.

I still have a vivid memory of the president as he described the episode. It was hardly what I would call a recollection in tranquillity. He sat forward in his chair; his face was flushed.

"I had all I could do to keep from exploding," he said. "The secretary was not to be disturbed but it was all right to disturb the president. I said a few harsh words to the young man on the other end of the phone and hung up. I went back to the game but it was no use. I was churning up inside. I was angry with Foster. I was angry with myself for having spoken harshly to the young man. He had made a mistake in judgment but I'm afraid I landed on him too heavily. It would probably be his only direct conversation with the president in his career. But I had chewed him out and hung up.

"I began to spray my shots over the golf course," the president said. "It was no use. I put my clubs in the bag and went back to the clubhouse. I began to ache all over. I didn't sleep very well. The next day I had my heart attack.

"I am not saying that Foster Dulles had his name on that heart attack but I can't help thinking of the incident that preceded it."

It was not surprising to me that, with the death of Dulles in 1959, and the departure of Sherman Adams as his top aide for domestic affairs, Eisenhower had come into his own as president. The pressures from all sides were no less omnipresent and difficult than before, but he discovered he had the capacity to deal with them directly.

In the early years of office, Eisenhower had felt alienated, sidelined. Now, he had new feelings of purpose and confidence; but his term of office was coming to an end and he knew the liabilities of being a lame duck. Even so, he was determined to make the most of the limited time remaining in his presidency. Beyond that, as he said earlier, he had robust anticipations of working for world peace as an ex-president. He hoped to be able to put to work some things he might have learned in the White House without having to worry about the multiplicity of restraints, given the wide array of forces involved in the making and implementing of policy.

What, I asked the president at the October 1960 meeting, were the most onerous of these restraining forces?

First of all, he said, there were those who seemed to worship complexity. They seemed to distrust anything that appeared to be open and direct. Nothing in the world was what it appeared to be. They fed on convoluted theories and had their antennae up for anything that smacked of conspiracy. They would speak about keeping presidential options open, by which they generally meant that they felt the president should take provocative actions or initiatives just to keep the other side off balance and to demonstrate he couldn't be taken for granted.

"I think you know that I believe we must be strong militarily," he said, "but beyond a certain point military strength can become a national weakness. The trouble with collecting military strength beyond our needs is that it tends to become a substitute for all the other things involved in true national security. It fosters the notion that national security is automatically tied to the amount of money spent on arms. What we overlook is that we may be spending our money on the wrong things. When we get into over-spending we get into misspending and inefficiencies. I don't want people who have a financial stake in crisis and tensions to have a voice in national policy."

There are many elements in true national security, the president continued, apart from weapons production. He referred, for example, to the need for public support for efforts to create a durable peace. He recognized the difficulty of creating such support, but was appalled at the way some of his government advisers would dismiss or downgrade this aspect of responsible government. And, even when they did agree to take it into account, they would usually do so by devising formulations or cover stories. The feeling seemed to be that the American people weren't intelligent enough to understand or deal with foreign policy; government was justified, therefore, in concocting cover stories. The president said he sometimes had to wonder whether he himself was getting the straight story.

Nothing was more important, he said, than determining how much military strength was necessary for national security, and he certainly appreciated the logic of a certain margin. But some people who benefited from military spending were not above exploiting world tensions in every way they could. He noticed that every time there appeared to be a good chance that tensions could be reduced, all sorts of reasons were advanced for turning away from those opportunities.

One of the inner-council arguments pressed on him for increasing military spending, he said, had nothing to do with the state of our defenses. According to this argument, we should step up the arms race as a form of economic warfare against the Soviet Union. The more we spent, he was told, the greater would be the pressure on the Soviet economy. Since the Soviet Union had no choice but to try to keep up with us in the arms competition, it would be forced to take money away from the domestic sector, thus producing dissatisfaction among the people even as it threatened the economic stability of the nation.

He was not taken in by this argument, for he knew it was generally the rationale for larger military budgets. What was most appalling about this approach was that it ignored the fact that unlimited military spending probably posed even more of a threat to our own economy and our social and political institutions than it did to those of the Soviet Union.

We discussed the opportunity presented by his Farewell Address, not far off, to talk sense to the American people, and he invited me to send him some notes for that occasion. I did in fact send a draft, but none of it was used. The talk as delivered was authentic Ike. Anyone who took the trouble to compare that "military-industrial complex" speech with his statement in 1952 before the first presidential campaign—a statement giving reasons why it was necessary to maintain a wall of separation between politics and the military—could see that both speeches came off the same spool. "Disarmament, with mutual honor and confidence, is a continuing imperative," he declared. "Together, we must learn how to compose differences, not with arms, but with intellect and decent purpose."

The response to the Farewell Address, at the time, was not resounding. In the years since that time, however, it has loomed increasingly large as a major American document. Certainly it has played an important part in the progressive reevaluation upward of his presidency.

When I visited General Eisenhower in his retirement at his farm in Gettysburg in 1964, his popularity was already returning to something approaching his wartime standing. He spoke only briefly about politics during our meeting. At Mamie's suggestion, he showed me some of his latest paintings, then spoke enthusiastically about techniques in mixing colors. "I know I'm no Churchill," he said with a grin.

Not much was said that day about the arms race, but he asked about the status of the Dartmouth Conferences, of which he had been the prime mover. He seemed especially pleased at the friendly tone of the discussions. He said that anyone who knew anything about the stockpiles of nuclear weapons knew that the only security for us, or for anyone else, was in bringing them under control and in maintaining the peace. And there was no option except to negotiate genuinely and energetically toward that end.

The legacy of Dwight D. Eisenhower to the American people may not be fully understood or used but it is still there for anyone who wants to put it to work. His warnings in the Farewell Address have particular meaning in the light of the circumstances leading up to the First World War, as described in the two books discussed in the next chapter.

6

Unremembered History

T wo books published in the 1930s described the role of the arms industry in fomenting tensions among nations and helping to set the stage for the First World War: *Merchants of Death* by H. C. Engelbrecht and F. C. Hanighen and *The Private Manufacture of Arms* by Philip Noel-Baker. The disclosures of profiteering through international traffic in weapons had a powerful effect on world public opinion. In the United States, there was a consensus that the sale of weapons should be rigorously controlled and the profit taken out of their manufacture.

The evidence in these books was incontrovertible that companies sold weapons to both sides, buying off government officials, and using the power of their profits to influence foreign policies. Some of the most colorful and incriminating passages in the two books dealt with the great armaments firms—among them Krupp, Du Pont, Vickers, Bethlehem Steel, and the lesser Colt, Remington, and Winchester companies—and with the agents and supersalesmen-at-large they hired to advance their interests. Noel-Baker, who won the Nobel Peace Prize, contended that there would always be prime obstacles to world peace until the manufacture of weapons was removed from private hands, and carried on by nonprofit, government-managed arsenals.

Noel-Baker quoted the eminent Lord Welby, Britain's principal Permanent Secretary to the Treasury: "We are in the hands of an organization of crooks. They are generals, politicians, manufacturers of armaments and journalists. All of them are anxious for unlimited expenditure, and go on inventing war scares to terrify the public and to terrify the Ministers of the Crown."

Another Noel-Baker quote, from a 1934 message sent to Congress by President Franklin D. Roosevelt: "The peoples of many countries are being taxed to the point of poverty and starvation . . . to enable governments to engage in a mad race in armaments . . . This grave menace to the peace of the world is due in no small measure to the uncontrolled activities of the manufacturers and merchants of engines of destruction, and it must be met by the concerted action of the peoples of all nations."

Finally, from the 1919 League of Nations Covenant: "The members of the League agree that the Manufacture by Private Enterprise of munitions and implements of war is open to grave objections." The people who drafted this Declaration included President Woodrow Wilson; Gen. Jan Smuts, Prime Minister of South Africa; Lord Robert Cecil, a major British Foreign Office official; Italian Prime Minister Vittorio Emanuele Orlando; and Greece's Prime Minister Eleutherios Venizelos.

Six "objections . . . to untrammelled private arms manufacture" were cited by the Temporary Mixed Commission, an investigating body set up by the League of Nations in the early 1920s (it was called "mixed" because its members were drawn from many different fields, including arms manufacture).

In shortened form, the six "objections" were that in the years leading to World War I, armament firms (1) fomented war scares in their own countries and abroad; (2) bribed government officials at home and abroad; (3) circulated false, inflammatory reports on various nations' military strength, to stimulate arms spending; (4) influenced public opinion by controlling certain newspapers and magazines; (5) played countries off against one another; and (6) organized international arms trusts that pushed up the price of arms.

The most publicized of the armaments supersalesmen was the ineffable "mystery man of Europe," Sir Basil Zaharoff, a shadowy figure who for many decades turned up in various countries stirring up unrest in order to hawk armaments made by the British munitions firm of Vickers. Sir Basil was the embodiment of George Bernard Shaw's *Major Barbara* character Andrew Undershaft, a munitions czar whose credo was to "give arms to all men who offer an honest price for them, without respect of persons or principles."

When, in the late 1800s, Zaharoff was representing the Scandinavian arms firm of Nordenfeldt, he sold to Greece—the country of his mother's birth—one of the first commercially available military submarines. The Greek high command was jubilant—until it came out that the wily Zaharoff had then gone to the Greeks' blood enemies, the Turks, had stampeded them into a panic about the menacing new Greek submarine, and had sold them *two* submersibles (along with other heavy armament).

When the American-born inventor Hiram Maxim demonstrated his remarkable new machine gun at a proving ground near Vienna, in the 1880s, Emperor Franz-Joseph himself was in the distinguished crowd of potential purchasers. So was Zaharoff, still representing the Nordenfeldt Company. Maxim's gun, which fired 666 bullets a minute, awed the onlookers by blowing away the dead center of several targets. Maxim then finished off in bravura fashion by neatly stitching the emperor's initials, FJ, onto the target. Whereupon, the story goes, Zaharoff shouldered his way through the crowd saying, "Marvellous! Nobody can compete with this *Nordenfeldt* gun!" He also said, convincingly but wrongly, that the Maxim gun was much too complicated to work well in combat. At least some of those present were apparently taken in by this crude tactic, for Maxim's sales fell off noticeably for some time after.

When Zaharoff was later employed by the British arms giant Vickers, he turned up in most of the world's trouble spots, wheeling, dealing, and playing one side off against the other. He was, in fact, so good at stirring up trouble—and thus landing huge armaments orders—that he was knighted by the British, even though he lived in France. In 1908, and again in 1913, the French government awarded him its Legion of Honor, for unspecified "services rendered." This "merchant of death" owned large blocks of stock in most of the world's armaments firms, and was considered fully as wealthy and influential as America's Rockefellers and Morgans.

Zaharoff was not only a supersalesman but also something of a lobbyist, propagandist, and secret agent. But American William B. Shearer, in the years following World War I, was strictly a specialist —he was a covert propagandist in the pay of Bethlehem Steel, Newport News Shipbuilding, and other armaments giants. Shearer's assignment, on instructions from his employers, was to undermine peace-and-disarmament initiatives. Before getting into this line of employment, Shearer was a fight promoter and nightclub manager.

Character assassination was one of the most lethal arrows in Shearer's quiver. One American shipbuilder, Brown Boveri, paid him handsomely to carry out attacks, complete with anonymous pamphlets and brochures, on the patriotism of such peace and disarmament figures as Dr. Nicholas Murray Butler, President of Columbia University, and Charles Evans Hughes, who was to become chief justice of the U.S. Supreme Court. Shearer's propaganda charged that Hughes had "betrayed America" by favoring arms control. The shocked readers of Shearer's pamphlets did not realize, of course, that they had been paid for by armaments firms.

Concurrently, Shearer had many other "arrangements": He was paid $2,000 a month to propagandize against the World Court and the League of Nations. To this end, he organized and stirred up patriotic groups, usually citing "documentary proof of a colossal conspiracy against the United States." In the process, he never passed up a chance to throw in denunciations of the perfidious British—a tactic designed, as he later frankly put it, "to fool the simple Irish" and enlist them as a constituency.

The highlight of Shearer's career came in 1927 when the Bethlehem Steel and Newport News Shipbuilding companies paid him $25,000 for six weeks of work. His assignment was to undermine the disarmament-minded Naval Conference convened that year in Geneva by President Calvin Coolidge. Sweeping into Geneva (seat of the League of Nations) Shearer set up shop as a purveyor of expertise on things naval. Nobody seemed quite sure who he was, but he entertained lavishly and was accepted as someone eminent because so many of the American officials present visibly deferred to him, and recommended him to journalists as an expert on the problems of naval disarmament. Soon newspapermen, statesmen, and most of the U.S. naval delegation were being "posted" by Shearer on the sinister implications of arms limitation. He was, as *Merchants of Death* put it, "the lion of the conference."

When the naval conference ended in failure, Noel-Baker later wrote, the *New York Times* correspondent Wythe Williams "sent a message [to his paper] in which he said that Mr. Shearer was 'openly exultant' . . . the following day . . . one of the leading Geneva papers ran an article about Shearer under the headline 'The Man Who Wrecked the Conference.'" Shearer, according to *Merchants of Death,* "took the trouble to clip [the story] and send it home to his backers."

Philip Noel-Baker downplayed Shearer's boast that he wrecked the conference single-handedly. But Noel-Baker did say that Shearer's propaganda "reacted . . . disastrously on the work of the conference. It injected into the proceedings an element of mistrust and passion which Geneva . . . had never known . . . the whole atmosphere was poisoned . . . he helped to create the atmosphere in which chief delegates find it hard to make concessions . . . But . . . Shearer was an instrument and nothing more . . . The people who must bear the blame are the Private Manufacturers of Arms who, to increase their profits, paid for his propaganda to defeat the Disarmament Treaty . . ."

Histories of arms races abound in such cases. In 1907, a German munitions representative, Paul von Gontard, pulled off a "gingering up" coup that armaments people spoke of glowingly for years afterward. Gontard placed articles in three influential French newspapers—*Figaro, Le Matin,* and *Echo de Paris*—proclaiming the virtues of a new machine gun the French army was supposedly buying by the thousands. Gontard then got one of his men in the German government to wave these articles in the faces of Reichstag members and demand strong counteraction. Stampeded, the Reichstag in the next few years spent—much of it with Gontard's firm—some $10 million on new machine guns. "Whatever the French may have planned to do before this increased preparation by Germany," Noel-Baker comments, "they were, of course, obliged thereafter to follow suit. A race in machine guns between France and Germany had thus been successfully begun."

True to their internationalist code, the arms makers seldom hesitated to make sales that might hurt their own countries. A famous case of selling to the enemy came to light during World War I at Verdun ("The bloodiest battle in history"). As Noel-Baker tells it, the Germans "left . . . the flower of their troops hanging on the enemy wire. The wire that held them up was not made in France . . . it came from Germany through Switzerland to Verdun two months before the battle had begun." Needless to say, the German manufacturers must have had a good idea of where the wire was headed and what it would be used for. What with all the prewar international armaments sales, most of the World War I belligerents found themselves facing rifle, cannon, and warship assaults undertaken with materiel originating in their own countries.

Indeed, one astounding sidelight of World War I was the way private firms on both sides traded vigorously with the enemy, through neutral countries. When the Germans ran short of vegetable oils and fats needed in the making of explosives, merchants from Britain obligingly forwarded cargoes of the needful to them through Denmark. International borders became similarly porous when, later in the war, the Fatherland needed such strategic metals as copper, nickel and lead, and bauxite (used to make aluminum for Germany's marauding subs). For her part, Germany supplied France, via Switzerland, with iron and steel in amounts of up to 250,000 tons per month. France, in turn, sold the Germans— through the ever-understanding Swiss—shipments of bauxite and carbide-cyanamide (a chemical used in making gunpowder).

Merchants of Death says that the Swiss sold Germany annually enough saltpeter to make "56 billion rifle [bullets] or 147 million hand grenades . . . The profits of this war traffic . . . were colossal.

Swiss aid to both belligerents . . . undoubtedly did much to prolong the war."

Meanwhile, even before we entered the war, American firms were also waxing fat by supplying arms to the Allies—despite President Wilson's call for neutrality. In the course of the war, Du Pont's stock shot up from $20 to $1000 a share. According to Engelbrecht and Hanighen, J. P. Morgan "was said to have made more money in two years than the elder Morgan made in all his life." (The elder Morgan had himself become one of the world's richest men—partly through buying defective rifles at $3 apiece and then selling them, unrepaired, to Gen. John C. Fremont, during the Civil War. President Lincoln said that those profiteering in defective weapons "ought to have their devilish heads shot off.")

Allied munitions purchases from America in the war amounted to $4 billion. If you add "nonwar" materials, Allied purchases from the U.S. during the period from August 1914 through February 1917 exceeded $10 billion.

In this euphoric atmosphere, profiteering—according to Federal Trade Commission studies—was commonplace. Du Pont, which supplied 40 percent of the Allies' ammunition needs, charged our government about fifty cents a pound for gunpowder that it produced at thirty-six cents a pound. The firm's annual profits, which before the war had been about six million, averaged about $58 million during the hostilities.

When it came to manipulating public opinion, American arms dealers were far behind the Krupps of Germany in World War I. The Krupp arms dynasty dated from the early 1800s. When Krupp's cannon far outperformed the French artillery in the Franco-Prussian War of 1870, all the world—the Chinese navy included—lined up for Krupp ordnance. Whenever supplies lagged behind in demand, Krupp arranged for the licensing of his patents. In the case of armor plating, Krupp charged royalties of $45 per ton. By 1912, Krupp was selling half of its products abroad.

From the onset of its major, post-1870 phase, Krupp found it prudent to co-opt the government, the nobility, the military, and the public. Three major German newspapers were under Krupp control.

It was easy enough to move public opinion in favor of big Krupp contracts. Bribes and payoffs ensured that the army and navy brass would push Krupp's products.

As for the government, the Krupps might well have said, with Bernard Shaw's Andrew Undershaft (and Louis XIV), "I *am* your government." When the Austro-Prussian war loomed in 1866, Prussia's legendary Iron Chancellor Count Otto von Bismarck urged Krupp to turn down the Austrian government's arms orders. Krupp calmly refused and delivered the guns with impunity. Noel-Baker quotes a Krupp contemporary: "Krupp employs hundreds of officers on leave or unattached, at a high salary for doing nothing very much. For some families Krupp's factory is a great sinecure where the nephews and poor relations of officials, whose influence in war is great, find themselves jobs."

Inevitably, the Krupps befriended the kaisers themselves. At the turn of the century the Navy-loving Kaiser Wilhelm II was, according to Engelbrecht and Hanighen, "not only a close friend of the Krupps, but he was godfather to Krupp's daughter Bertha [after whom the giant World War I cannon "Big Bertha" was named]. Wilhelm arranged Bertha's marriage to Count von Bohlen, he took his whole court to attend Frau Krupp's great balls, and he often spoke of Krupp as his business 'partner.' " Like so many other German government and military notables of his time, the kaiser owned large blocks of Krupp stock, and so had a deep-running interest in maintaining the firm's good health. *Merchants of Death* sums up the situation well: "The German government was encouraging and establishing an alien kingdom in the heart of Germany, a power which it could not control, yet could not do without."

Krupps had no monopoly, of course, on cozy relationships with top-drawer power figures. "The British government," Noel-Baker observes, "has, it is probably true to say, given more knighthoods to Directors of Armaments firms than to representatives of all the rest of British industry put together."

Typically, the boards of British arms companies fairly bristled with titles and Big Names: dukes, barons, members of Parliament, naval officers, strategically placed publishers—even bishops! Lord Philip Snowden, chancellor of the exchequer, said before Britain's House of Commons, ". . . I find that honorable members in this House are very largely concerned [with arms firms]. Indeed, it would be impossible to throw a stone on the benches opposite without hitting a member who is a shareholder in one or another of these firms."

If this was the situation in England's Mother of Parliaments, one can only wonder what went on elsewhere. But even with such heavy backing in high places, the arms industry felt it necessary, occasionally, to boost its sales by stirring up war scares. One such was the "Big Navy" scare of 1909, also called the Mulliner Panic. Mr. H. H. Mulliner—not to be confused with the famous P. G. Wodehouse character of the same last name—was managing director of Britain's Coventry Ordnance Works. A vociferous self-proclaimed patriot, he began leaking to the sensational press all manner of alarming stories about Germany's "buildup" of its dreadnought fleet. Much later on, the stories were shown to have been wrong, but by then the damage had long since been done. In 1909, however, a Mulliner-inspired British general told a shocked House of Lords about the German "buildup," warning that "a terrible awakening is in store for us at no distant date." A demand for new battleships arose under the slogan, "We want eight and we won't wait." In the end, four battleships were commissioned, and Mulliner's firm profited handsomely.

Clearly, H. H. Mulliner did not bring off his dreadnought coup by himself: A widespread arms constituency was already out there waiting for him, *wanting* to believe that Germany was a growing menace. But was it? True, Germany did have its "tiger," High Adm. Alfred von Tirpitz, who was forever framing Naval Laws and demanding that the Reichstag underwrite new naval buildups. Further, Kaiser Wilhelm himself was a passionate Big-Navy buff.

Britain produced its own "Von Tirpitz," the fire-breathing First Sea Lord Admiral John "Hell-Jack" Fisher. To the delight of the arms makers, Hell-Jack was gung ho for a naval buildup directed at the Germans. *Merchants of Death* quotes armaments manufacturer Sir Charles D. Maclaren, speaking to a meeting of his stockholders:

"The appointment of Sir John Fisher at the Admiralty is a fact of some importance to a firm like ours . . . I am glad to see Sir John is prepared to go in for building battleships, because the heavier the work, the more of it goes to our firm . . . when heavy work is about, we will get our share of it."

Above all, Hell-Jack pinned his hopes on construction of 18,000-ton battleships, which he regarded as a sort of floating Maginot line shielding England from the Hun. The first such vessel—the *Dreadnought,* launched in 1906—was a steam turbine-driven monster with twice the firepower of earlier warships. Thereafter, *all* super-battleships were called dreadnoughts.

The arrival of the dreadnought produced unforeseen repercussions. For the long run, Fisher's conversion of the fleet from coal to oil put the British square into the politics of Middle Eastern oil, for decades to come. But more immediately, the new dreadnought lineup scared the Germans mightily. Their reaction, however, was *not* to cringe and give way to Britain. Instead, they plunged feverishly into a naval counter-buildup of their own.

The pattern evident in this British-German naval rivalry runs like a red thread through all of modern history; a war scare touches off an arms buildup; the buildup is matched or topped by the enemy's counter-buildup; which only leads the first side to . . . Thus, the introduction of Maxim's machine gun prompted development of a counter-weapon, the tank, which was designed to wipe out machine-gun nests. The tanks, in turn, bred a new generation of awesome tank-killer weapons. Or, again, during the pre-World War I jockeying for position, the French—egged on by armaments propagandists—gave Russia a huge loan with the stipulation that it should be used only for arms and for the construction of strategic railroads leading to the German frontier. The Russians, depleted by losing the 1904–1905 war with Japan, accepted the loan with alacrity. This bold move gave the edgy Germans a strong reason for attacking Russia.

In such charged, quiveringly balanced situations, energetic mischief-making by the arms firms has often been the feather-on-the-scale that tipped things toward war. Arms makers may not have caused wars from the ground up, but they have often helped to supply the crucial push. Further, the munitions makers seemed unable to resist tampering with the political structure of their own countries—as when Krupp, Thyssen, and other arms firms gave strategic support to the nascent Nazi movement.

In 1934, the U.S. Senate investigated the activities of armaments manufacturers. An exchange took place between Senator Joel Clark of Missouri, and Lawrence Spear, vice-president of the Electric Boat Company of New York. Herewith, a portion of the transcript:

SENATOR CLARK: Did you regard it as a calamity when the United States State Department was able to bring about the resumption of diplomatic relations between Peru and Chile, and prevent a war?

MR. SPEAR: I certainly regarded at the time it would have a bad influence on our negotiations. [Electric Boat had been trying to sell both sides submarines.]

SENATOR CLARK: You regarded the activities of the State Department in attempting to preserve peace and improve diplomatic activities as pernicious?

MR. SPEAR: That is the word I used.

The unflappable Mr. Spear figured in another revelation brought out by the Senate Committee. In 1924, Spear had received a letter from a Peruvian ex-navy commander named Luis Aubry, who was a full-time employee of Electric Boat. Aubry was a specialist at "gingering up" Latin American governments and bribing their officials. The letter read, "I am planning to be appointed by the Government, if you permit, delegate for Peru in the Disarmament Conference that is going to take place in Geneva in June, 1925. I feel that I can do something good . . . for the cause of submarines in South America . . . I require your authorization . . ."

Spear consulted his superior, Henry Carse, who generously okayed the leave of absence—so that his ace submarine salesman could sit amidst a delegation of his countrymen at a disarmament conference! In 1934, Carse, with a straight face, insisted to the Senate Committee that, in okaying Aubry's cat-among-the-pigeons assignment, "We were not taking any part in attempting to influence a world conference . . ."

Spear's attempts to undercut his own government's "pernicious" peace diplomacy in South America seem to have done his career no harm. In the end Carse and his industry easily rode out the storm attendant on the Senate Committee revelations.

During the 1930s, Du Pont put out a handsome booklet extolling the Army and Navy and making the point, over and over, that "Du Pont has been inseparably connected with combat history in every organization in the service." The booklet was sent gratis to every officer in the U.S. Armed Forces. It was almost made to appear that one was unpatriotic if he or she was an advocate of government, rather than private, manufacture of arms.

Did these firms really believe that government yards were unable to do decent work? That seems unlikely, since a few government shipyards were even then building, among other war vessels, perfectly serviceable submarines. This fact got little publicity from the newspapers, and of course none at all from the private firms irked by this competition.

In the late 1920s, Sir Charles Craven of Vickers-Armstrong wrote in a letter to Lawrence Spear of Electric Boat: "I wish you the best of luck and hope you may be able to knock out some of your Government dockyards. They seem to be more of a nuisance with you than they are here."

Even among themselves, the manufacturers stoutly maintained the pretense that they opposed government manufacture of arms only because they felt the product would be of inferior quality. In a 1935 speech before the annual general meeting of the Fairey Aviation Company of Britain, Mr. C. R. Fairey said, "only our highly specialized industry is capable of fulfilling the . . . requirements . . . the effort to obtain the necessary aircraft . . . by organizing national factories would fail . . . they could not possibly acquire our knowledge and technique . . ."

The crowning irony here is that the very companies which professed such contempt for government technology were only too eager to appropriate and put to use the findings of government research labs. They enjoyed, free, the fruits of research done at institutions that cost the taxpayers millions to maintain.

When the details of these ugly situations were finally dug out in the 1920s and 1930s by various arms control conferences and investigations, they were collected and made available to the larger public by *Merchants of Death* and *The Private Manufacture of Arms.* These books were "lightning rods," prime factors in creating the climate of opinion that by the late 1930s was strongly unfavorable to the private arms makers.

A half-century later, this history is all but forgotten. The traffic in arms in today's world differs from its predecessors in World War I in several respects. First of all, the "merchants of death" of earlier days are no longer the primary sellers. In today's world, the sales are carried out by government itself. Salesmen representing the Pentagon travel the world, pressing the merits of American weapons in competition with salesmen from other governments, whether Britain or France or Israel or the Soviet Union. Since the early 1980s, all patterns of restraint in the international sale of arms have disappeared. Military "assistance" has become an extension of the domestic military buildup. It represents an effort to channel political leverage and influence away from the Soviet Union. One of the prime arguments for the promotion of arms sales is that the income is necessary to reduce both the American balance of payments deficit and the costs of U.S. defense production (e.g., through cost-sharing and selling of surplus output). What is most disturbing about the practice is that questions of moral principle, which at one time were held to be central in American policy, have hardly been raised.

In addition to policy, other aspects of the international sale of arms have changed. At one time, the U.S. government shunned sales of arms to nations other than allies because of national security reasons. Today, anyone can buy—and even those who can't "pay" are given highly favorable terms. The Third World has provided the "best" customers, most of them in the Middle East. The old taboos against selling arms in highly volatile situations have been scotched. So have policies against providing highly advanced technology to potential foes. Now we have pressure selling of a wide range of sophisticated weaponry and technological know-how.

The United States and the Soviet Union are the world's leading

arms suppliers—each furnishing a third of the world's arms sales—
with France, Britain, West Germany, and Italy comprising the majority of the balance. From 1971 to 1980, the U.S. sold $97.6 billion
worth of arms to foreign nations—approximately eight times the
amount for the preceding two decades. In the period from 1979 to
1983, the United States collected over $40 billion in its weapons sales
to seventy-three countries. As Senator Hubert Humphrey once observed, America has become "a kind of arms supermarket into
which any customer can walk and pick up whatever he wants."

Through six administrations, the United States has proclaimed
a policy seeking to pacify the Middle East. Yet arms sales from the
U.S. to Saudi Arabia, Jordan, and Kuwait, have amounted to nearly
$45 billion, making it necessary for Israel to seek ever-higher com-
mitments of war material from the United States. During the period
from 1979 to 1983, the Middle East was the world's largest recipient
of arms, with equipment supplied by all the major world munitions
makers. Sales of arms abroad have been integral to Pentagon policy
and planning. The primary beneficiaries have been the American
arms manufacturers; yet the American taxpayers have had to absorb
the costs of promoting and negotiating such sales. "Arms sales are
the hard currency of foreign affairs," a senior State Department
official observed in 1982. "They replace the security pacts of the
1950s."

Virtually unrestricted international arms trafficking is not without its consequences. The sale of weapons has stimulated arms races
between bordering nations—exacerbating tensions and encouraging
the quest for increasingly destructive military solutions to political
disputes. The sellers show no inhibitions about creating tensions that
can result in hostilities and spread to neighboring countries.

Arms sold to other countries are not always used in ways that
conform to the given assurances. Commitments obtained from a
"client" nation are no guarantees of compliance, as demonstrated by
the peace-keeping records of the recipients of American arms over
the past ten years. Increases in recklessness parallel the growth of
power. In some case, recipients have used American weapons to
destroy the freedoms we say we want to support. Iran served as one

of the most bitter lessons. All that Americans had to show for the billions of dollars committed to Iran in the sixties was a staunchly anti-American sentiment following the removal of the shah.

Because of the stiff competition from other foreign arms suppliers, domestic companies have pushed harder for international clients. Senate committee records show that foreign officials have been bribed to buy our war merchandise. Corporate financial entanglements make it difficult for the U.S. government to extricate itself from unhealthy political ties. Some U.S. arms manufacturers have developed a strong dependency on foreign arms sales.

The net effect of the arms traffic is to strengthen the role of the arms lobby in the economic and political life of the nation. The additional muscle given to the arms establishment through heavy appropriations is not absent in foreign policy, which in turn fosters larger military budgets. The cycle was perhaps best described by John Foster Dulles, Secretary of State: "In order to bring a nation to support the burdens of maintaining great military establishments, it is necessary to create an emotional state akin to war psychology. There must be the portrayal of external menace. This involves the development to a high degree of the nation-hero, nation-villain ideology and the arousing of the population to a sense of sacrifice. Once these exist, we have gone a long way on the path to war."

7

The Whistle-Blowers

If the post-World War I generation had its Engelbrechts and Hanighens and Noel-Bakers who wrote about abuses and dangers connected to the private manufacture of armaments, the present generation can look to a small but dedicated group equally intent on informing the public about the way the term "national security" is being used as a facade for excessive and careless military spending. Among the current crop of sentries are four individuals. They work together, but each of them has his or her own special station and vantage point. They have won for themselves the name of "Whistle-Blowers."

I. Senator Charles Grassley

Senator Charles Grassley, Republican of Iowa, is hardly what one would regard as a typical foe of the "military-industrial establishment." He is an Iowa farmer—lean, lanky, slow-talking—who looks as though he had been hired to play the part of Jimmy Stewart in an update of *Mr. Smith Goes to Washington*. He is well over six feet but is anything but overbearing in manner and posture, stooping most of the time to get closer to the eye level of his visitors. His large hands are heavily veined and attest that they belong to no parlor farmer.

Grassley learned law-making at the local level, especially in the state legislature. He took readily to political conservatism, reflecting the views familiar to him since his childhood. He advanced steadily in politics and, in 1974, just turned forty, was elected to the House of Representatives. After three terms in the House, he waged a successful campaign for the U.S. Senate and was pleased when he was appointed to the Senate Budget Committee. Convinced that his constituents expected him to be a watchdog over government spending, he strongly supported President Ronald Reagan's demand for a balanced budget and cheered when the President called for a thoroughgoing effort to rid the government of waste and fraud. As a congressman, he had battled abuses in the Food Stamp program and applauded President Reagan when he called attention to double payments to some welfare recipients, but was puzzled when the President failed to demonstrate equal outrage over far more consequential evidence of waste and fraud in military spending.

The education of Charles Grassley progressed with reports of the General Accounting Office showing military over-spending, over-runs, and over-charging—and culminated in the realization that what the American people were buying was not so much a program for the defense of the United States as a system for funnelling massive public funds to private contractors.

An exchange with Franklin C. Spinney, a cost analyst for the Department of Defense, was an important factor in Grassley's emergence as a powerful Senate opponent to military misspending. Spinney had been quoted privately and publicly about extravagance and carelessness in the handling of Pentagon appropriations. Grassley phoned Secretary of Defense Caspar Weinberger and requested a meeting with Spinney. At first, Weinberger appeared willing, but changed his mind and ordered Spinney not to talk to Grassley. An irate Grassley got into his orange Chevette, drove over to the Pentagon, and challenged Weinberger directly. Within a month, Grassley had maneuvered, behind-the-scenes, an unprecedented forum—a joint hearing between the Senate Budget and Armed Services Committees—and summoned Spinney to testify. What was an otherwise routine budget briefing became a dramatic hearing before eight TV cameras and hordes of national press that made the cover of *Time* magazine.

Spinney's testimony before the Senate Committee was forthright and dramatic. Under careful questioning, Spinney calmly and methodically reported his direct knowledge of Pentagon budget abuses. There emerged from his replies an astonishing account of irresponsibility in the handling of government funds. Senator Grassley came to realize that Spinney's recital was only a glimmering of a vast government scandal. While it may have lacked the conspiratorial character of the notorious Teapot Dome frauds of the early twenties, it pointed to much larger losses by American taxpayers.

The picture that took shape from Grassley's probing was far more alarming than fifteen-cent nuts and bolts that cost the taxpayers $25 each, or a hammer worth $8 for which we paid $435, or $8 pliers costing us $745, or a $125 coffee brewer costing us $7,600, or a $700 sofa that went for $15,000. Some of these items were bought in bulk, which translated into millions of dollars of over-spending —assuming the excessive costs were a matter of over-spending and not of fraud.

At first, Senator Grassley was inclined to believe that the significance and prevalence of these items had been grossly exaggerated. In any large-scale spending program, freakish incidents were bound to turn up. Nothing was easier or more unfair than to hold up a $435 hammer in front of a television camera and condemn the total program of the Department of Defense. As Senator Grassley dug into Pentagon accounts, however, he realized that the expensive hammers and sofas could not be dismissed as oddities. They were the result of systematic and exorbitant pricing formulas used by major defense contractors not only for hammers and pliers but for ships, tanks, planes, and almost everything else bought by the Pentagon. They were integral to a system designed for maximum expenditure of public funds and maximum profit to suppliers. It was difficult for Senator Grassley to avoid the conclusion that the United States was fast becoming a military welfare state.

The disclosure of the $435 hammer was only the symbolic beginning of a long trail of waste, overlapping, redundancy, and inefficiency that kept spiraling upward until it affected the organization of the defense of the United States. At the bottom of the spiral were the spending policies—the absence of genuine "competitive" bidding and absurd amounts paid for defense items. On the way to the top of the spiral were questionable decisions about the kinds of weapons that would have an essential place in a rational and competent defense program. And at the top was the foreign policy itself. If the weapons manufacturers played such a large part in Pentagon decision-making, was it illogical to believe that they were without influence in matters of foreign policy? To what extent was genuine arms control being frustrated not just by difficulties in negotiations but by the need to keep the arms race going as an end in itself? To what extent was the ability to make correct assessments about threats and challenges confronting the United States affected not just by the actions of the Soviet Union but by the need to maintain tensions as a rationale for a massive military spending program?

Devising a sound program for the national defense required not just scrupulous buying policies but a sound approach to the total structure of peace-making. The factor of waste in the way hammers or coffee pots or tanks or planes were bought could actually affect the way we protected ourselves as a nation.

Where to start in dealing with this upward spiral? Senator Grassley was not on the Senate Foreign Relations Committee. But as a member of the Budget Committee he had an opportunity to scrutinize the total defense program. Was decision-making about weapons overly influenced by private pressures? When tanks were being bought, were we buying the best tanks or the most expensive ones? When fighter planes were ordered, were we giving as much attention to their place in the total portfolio of our defense needs as we were to pressures of the airplane manufacturers? If we had submarines capable of delivering atomic explosives on as many military or civilian targets as might be itemized, why was it necessary to spend billions of dollars on other delivery systems, especially those that could be more readily identified and attacked by an enemy? If we already had a stockpile of more than 30,000 nuclear explosives, why was it necessary to continue to produce them at the rate of from seven to eight each day?

The military reality of nuclear explosives was that the United States possessed more than enough bombs to meet any conceivable destructive need; yet the atomic plants continued to spew them out almost as though the act of manufacture was a manifestation of our manhood. A man who is building a barn wants the sturdiest roof obtainable; yet he would be aghast if the contractor suggested a roof twenty feet thick. Why would we need upward of 30,000 nuclear bombs if only a fraction of that amount could lay waste to the entire world? At what point would we feel we had enough?

Questions such as these were involved in Grassley's probe. The twenty-foot-thick roof syndrome became apparent to him in the basic organization of the military forces. Obviously, the armed services had to consist of an army, navy, and air force; but it was equally obvious that each of the armed services regarded itself virtually as a total military operation.

In the 1940s, former President Herbert Hoover headed a commission to investigate the way the military defenses of the United States were organized. The report of the Hoover Commission called attention to a prodigious waste of resources, manpower, and money in the maintenance of what, in effect, was three separate military establishments. The extra costs were also reflected in the loss of military efficiency.

The Hoover Commission was followed by legislation in 1949 that provided for full unification of the armed forces of the United States under a single Department of Defense. Under the Unification Act, all three military branches would be responsible to a Secretary of Defense, although each branch would have its own civilian secretary. Coordination functions would be carried out through what would be called the Joint Chiefs of Staff. The organization chart showed the secretary of defense at the top, followed by the secretaries of the Army, Air Force, and Navy, and then the military chiefs of each branch. The Joint Chiefs would advise the president, the secretary of defense, and the National Security Council. The NSC would include representatives not just of the military but of the

Central Intelligence Agency, the State Department, the National Security Agency, and the White House staff itself.

What was intended as a streamlined plan for unification became more form than substance. For example, under unification, the U.S. Air Force became a fully formed independent unit, but the Army was allowed its own air capability. The Navy had to operate the aircraft off its carriers as well as to maintain auxiliary air services, and the Marines didn't want to be left out in the cold. In any case, the armed forces of the United States today are a long way from the fully integrated military organization that President Hoover envisioned in his report. The most obvious effect, of course, is to be found in overlapping budgets, duplicate functions, and even a competing psychology. Experts consulted by Senator Grassley estimated that all this redundancy costs the taxpayers something in excess of $30 billion a year.

Senator Grassley learned that one reason for runaway costs is the way the Department of Defense buyers circumvent the law requiring competitive bidding. True, the Pentagon would go through the procedures mandated by the Congress before awarding contracts. True, too, the contracts would generally go to the lowest bidder (which usually turned out to be the company favored by the Pentagon). However, after a short while, the company receiving the contract would send in revised estimates calling for whopping increases over the original bids, a practice called "buying-in," and had no trouble in receiving approval for the new schedules and contract prices. Under these circumstances, it was apparent to Senator Grassley that "competitive bidding" had become a sham. Little wonder that the cost experts consulted by Grassley estimated that, for every dollar being spent on defense acquisition, we were actually receiving only thirty cents in real value.

Grassley also discovered that hundreds of admirals and generals who were involved in awarding lush contracts would turn up later on the payrolls of weapons manufacturers who had benefited from their decisions. A seat in Congress, too, became a way station for dozens of ex-congressmen who had given full support to Pentagon budget requests. There was no law preventing military personnel or congressmen from going to work for private companies, but questions had to be asked when plush jobs went to officials who were involved in awarding contracts or voting for massive military spending.

All his political life, Charles Grassley had been a conservative, but he could not accept the notion that, in order to demonstrate his conservative credentials, he had to endorse a blank check to the order of private companies on the Treasury of the United States. He had no difficulty in deciding that his main mission in political life would be to combat the wanton giveaway of public funds—whatever the political price and however high the scandal might reach.

What about the fact of growing Soviet military power? Even if the American taxpayer was getting only thirty cents on the dollar in actual value, wasn't it risky to call attention to this fact in view of possible disruptions in our military program that might result from such startling disclosures? Grassley's initial support of Pentagon budget requests had been based on reports that the United States was at a growing military disadvantage alongside the Soviet Union. Accordingly, he had energetically supported the president's efforts to upgrade the national defenses. But he had cause to wonder whether tensions were not being exploited or manipulated in order to perpetuate and justify enlarged military spending. He wasn't sure whether the alarms being sounded about Soviet military superiority in certain areas were literally true or whether they had their primary origin in efforts to create a stage for yet higher military budgets.

Senator Grassley did not want to see the United States disadvantaged by new Soviet military advances or developments. But he began to realize that the military authorities in both the United States and Soviet Union were playing off each other. The easiest way, apparently, for the military in each nation to obtain increased funding and power was by presenting "authentic" new information about existing or projected new weapons developments by the other country. Usually, the standard argument was that the military could not be responsible for the national security unless it had unfettered authority to define and pursue its own requirements. The march of events, however, demonstrated that national security was decreased, not increased, when both sides competed in weapons development.

Another key argument Senator Grassley had to confront was that, where the safety of the United States was concerned, there should be no argument about costs. But he began to realize that American security was in jeopardy precisely because of the grip of the private companies on spending policies. Our defense program could be no better than the way it was administered.

President Eisenhower's warning to the American people about the military-industrial complex hit home. The term "military security" had become a shield behind which the American people were being systematically drained and defrauded. Grassley realized that people who couldn't be trusted to safeguard the national wealth could hardly be trusted to safeguard the national security. He saw no direct connection between the amount of money we were putting into defense and the amount of security we were getting in return.

The analysis of defense spending convinced Grassley that some sixty billion to eighty billion dollars could be cut from the military budget not only without detriment to actual security but with an actual strengthening in our defense posture. Only when we adopt a new yardstick for measuring value received will we know where we really stand in terms of the national defense. Certainly, nothing can be more risky to the economic health of the nation than a massive national debt, involving as it does long-term dislocations and inflationary pressures. Taking all these facts into account, Grassley persuaded his colleagues in the Senate to vote for a freeze on military spending pending a full review of military policies.

For example, why was it, Senator Grassley asked, that whenever Congress mandated certain limits on military spending, the Pentagon would cut back on virtually everything except orders going to the weapons contractors? Field forces might be cut, recruitment might be deferred—but the weapons manufacturers would continue to get their full share. Was the highest priority being given to the uninterrupted flow of money to the private companies? Why did Pentagon officials quickly learn that the surest way to advancement and personal power was through maximum spending? Why should such officials fear that the surest way to become dead-ended or downgraded was by opposing spending policies and practices? Why should questioners like Franklin Spinney find themselves muzzled by their superiors?

Members of Congress like Senator Grassley represent the best hope for reversing the shift in political and economic power to the military. However, nothing could be more unfair or inaccurate than to condemn all military officials because of the influence of the arms manufacturers over procurement policies. The overwhelming majority of those in the armed services—from enlisted men to the officers and the Joint Chiefs of Staff—are honest, intelligent, and dedicated to the service of the American people. Highly ranked officers like Gen. David Jones, former chairman of the Joint Chiefs of Staff, and former Adm. Noel Gaylor, recognized, as did President Eisenhower, that the security of the United States depends more on the control of force than on the pursuit of force in the world. Few political officials believed more deeply than did General Jones in the need for serious discussions with the Soviets on matters related both to arms control and the need to reduce tensions between the two countries. General Jones was not blind to Soviet purposes or strategy but also recognized that the USSR had as much of a stake in preventing a nuclear conflict as did the United States. In any event, the United States could not afford to overlook any opening, however slight, for genuine negotiations leading to arms reduction or control or both.

Granted that some members of the military believe in the need to create workable methods of averting war, what about the context in which such men have to function?

II. Rear Admiral Gene La Rocque

Following thirty-one years of service in the Navy, Adm. Gene La Rocque founded the Center for Defense Information, a nonprofit, nonpartisan organization devoted to the objective analysis of past and proposed military policy and the prevention of nuclear war.

Son of a well-to-do furniture merchant, La Rocque grew up in

Kankakee, Illinois. A simple advertisement urging "Join the Navy" launched him into what turned out to be an impressive naval career. While attending midshipman school at Northwestern University, he was honored as the outstanding student in a class of 1,200. After receiving his commission, he asked to be sent to Pearl Harbor because it "sounded romantic" and wound up aboard the U.S.S. *Mac-Donough* under fire from the Japanese. He spent the duration of World War II on fighting ships in the Pacific that were involved in thirteen major naval battles. He won a commendation medal for sinking a Japanese submarine. After the war, he remained in the Navy because he believed that the U.S. could prevent war by staying strong.

He taught at military colleges and served as a military analyst both in the office of the Chief of Naval Operations and with the Joint Chiefs of Staff. While at the Pentagon, he was awarded a Legion of Merit for his work in strategic planning.

With the nuclearization of U.S. military forces and with increasing preparations for fast military response to international crisis, La Rocque became convinced that the Clausewitzian notion of war as a continuation of foreign policy by military means was no longer workable. He realized there could be no winners in a nuclear war.

A related concern to him was the growing institutionalization of militarism in America. After World War II, the Joint Chiefs of Staff became an established institution. The National Security Council became a new feature of government, along with the CIA—the full operations of which were unreported to the American people in what La Rocque regarded as a violation of the U.S. Constitution. For the first time in America, he felt, the military had senior status to the civilian-controlled State Department.

La Rocque became increasingly apprehensive about the effect of the military establishment on American traditions, just as he had increasing doubts about the ability of military strength to prevent war. It seemed to him that the glorified memory of U.S. involvement in World War II had produced a dangerous tendency to think that almost any problem in the world would yield to our use of military force. He was struck by the tendency of the military to approach questions of national interest with superficial impressions or a priori analyses. He thought it significant that many of the men who advanced the most rapidly in military service were those who advocated an unlimited buildup of military force.

Yet along with these realizations, he knew that criticism from within was not very effective. He himself had disciplined a young officer for having questioned the need for the nuclear missiles they were carrying. He was convinced that systemic changes would have to come from outside the military establishment.

In 1966, La Rocque was asked by the secretary of the Navy, Paul Nitze, to head a task force of ten senior officers to study the Vietnam War and make recommendations for action. The question put to them: "What should the U.S. do?"

The team went to Vietnam. "We looked at all the options for completing that war," La Rocque recalled. "It became obvious that we were wasting kids without really knowing why. There were no real goals. And that was what I told General [William] Westmoreland, 'You're spending $90,000,000 a day . . . and you don't really know why.' " After nine months of research, the group concluded that there was absolutely no way that they could win the war in Vietnam, and advised Secretary of Defense Robert McNamara accordingly.

The report was not a hit. La Rocque said amiably that it didn't endear him to officialdom. It remained nameless and unpublished. Among the alienated was Chief of Naval Operations Admiral Thomas Moorer, later to become chairman of the Joint Chiefs of Staff.

"That's when the 'lateral transfers' began," La Rocque noted. Up until that point, his career had steadily headed upward. After several "lateral transfers" he realized that there was no future left for him with the Navy, so he began collecting material for an organization that he had long envisioned starting. The organization would independently evaluate the need for proposed and existing weapons systems and the use of military force from a national rather than a single-service perspective. He believed in a strong national defense, but, like General Eisenhower, recognized that national strength was equally dependent upon strong social, economic, and political policies. He saw the need for an organization dedicated to providing a rational basis for alternative military policies that would eliminate waste and reduce the danger of nuclear war. He initially called it the "Eisenhower Institute," in honor of the president whose unheeded warnings of the dangers inherent in the military-industrial complex had been a source of inspiration to him.

La Rocque dug into his new project—now called the Center for Defense Information (CDI)—lined up foundation money, rented space, and hired his first staff assistant, David Johnson, now Director of Research. The first activity of CDI was the regular publication of a bulletin under the title *The Defense Monitor*. It challenged the advertised validity of the Soviet naval buildup and the subsequent need for more American naval forces, opposing the case for more forces made by the chairman of the Joint Chiefs of Staff, Admiral Moorer. La Rocque's publication caught the attention of Senator William Proxmire, chairman of the Joint Economic Committee and relentless critic of military waste, who incorporated the Admiral's research into a speech that gave CDI national recognition.

Overnight, CDI was inundated with requests for information and interviews. La Rocque also believed that he had a lot of latent support within the services. "I got calls," he said, "from people I barely knew who are still in the Pentagon saying that what I am doing is a necessary thing and that the excessive expenditures, duplications, and unnecessary redundancy in our force levels need to be brought to light." A little over a decade later, CDI had acquired another retired rear admiral as its deputy director, and two major generals, a colonel, and a navy captain as full-time associate directors.

The Defense Monitor has developed into an influential journal, which monthly rebuts Defense Department assertions and exposes problems with weapons programs (e.g., the long-term consequences of MIRVs) often well in advance of their accepted validity. These reports analyze issues such as U.S.–Soviet military strength, the SALT agreements, U.S. military assistance programs, the B-1 Bomber, space weapons, nuclear weapons testing, and nuclear war.

"I am told by [former Nixon aide] Pat Buchanan, who happens to be my neighbor," boasted La Rocque, "that when President Nixon went to Moscow in 1973 he had on top of his stack of papers [*The Defense Monitor*'s] analysis of the strategic arms limitation talks. We took very complex sets of figures and reduced them to very simple formulas so that anybody could understand them. That is the sort of thing that even our political leaders need."

What makes CDI publications so reputable was best described by a representative of the Joint Committee on Defense Production: "They make their argument on the basis of military need. They'll tell you that the B-1 Bomber is bad because it costs too much and won't do the job, instead of that bombers are bad because they kill people." The fact that the experienced military officers who direct CDI are deeply concerned about the national interest lends credibility to their research findings.

In keeping with its commitment to objectivity, CDI will not accept any money from the government, or from military, industrial, political, or special interest groups. Neither military personnel on active duty nor anyone who has an axe to grind against the military are permitted to serve on the staff.

CDI's success is reflected in the ever-growing demand for its services. It has been cited several thousand times a year in major dailies and magazines across the nation and in military publications as well. The CDI staff routinely assists Congressional staffs with research, development of agenda, questions, and potential witness lists for hearings. It provides data for all the major government offices (e.g., the Office of Management and Budget); and occasionally, even the Pentagon has referred individuals to CDI for information that could not be obtained officially.

III. A. Ernest Fitzgerald

Ernest Fitzgerald, Air Force Management Systems Deputy (or in-house cost-cutter), has saved taxpayers millions of dollars through his frequent testimonies before congressional committees regarding cost abuses.

A native of Birmingham, Alabama, Fitzgerald served in the Navy during World War II and then earned his degree in industrial engineering from the University of Alabama in 1951. He spent the next fourteen years conducting cost analyses in the aerospace industry. Deeply troubled by the waste he had seen in weapons programs, in 1965 he accepted a $10,000 cut in salary to devote himself to official cost-cutting. He became aware that much of the waste had its origin in government-sanctioned policies and contractor schemes. Unlimited spending for weapons programs became the means by which the contractors had virtually unobstructed access to public funds. Fitzgerald was shocked that contractors would be reimbursed for expenses without documentation. He noticed that even during a period of relative price stability (e.g., 3 percent increases in industrial pay), typical labor outputs were 40 percent below competitive standards while pay rates and overhead costs were upwards of 50 percent. He saw that contractors with the worst records of meeting contractual commitments showed consistently above-average profits. In other words, at significantly higher costs, taxpayers were getting lower quality military hardware *and* less of it. In the name of national defense, our military capability and readiness were being impaired even as our ability to compete in the international market place was being reduced. Meanwhile, the public assumed that if military leaders wanted something they ought to have it. The result was overpriced junk, unconscionable profits, and reduced security.

Evidence that we were creating a military welfare state was to be found in Public Law 85-804, which holds that contractors who are "deemed essential" to national defense must be protected against bankruptcy. This means that American citizens are required to underwrite incompetence, waste, and even fraud. The Pentagon was given the power to subsidize suppliers who had broken their contractual obligations. National security had become the facade behind which the national treasury was being brazenly raided.

Finally, Fitzgerald found that the government's efforts to obtain *final* estimates of cost and schedule were meaningless. Nonbinding final estimates turned out to be a manifestation of what Fitzgerald termed the First Law of Program Management: "too early to tell and too late to stop."

In 1968, Senator Proxmire investigated the cost increases for the C-5A Transport plane, which were rumored to have gone up $2 billion apiece above the predicted price in a three-year period. As Air Force Management Systems Deputy, Fitzgerald was one of the several Pentagon officials asked to verify under oath to the Joint Economic Committee's Subcommittee on Economy in Government as to whether or not this was true. The Pentagon asked its witnesses to "play dumb," but apparently Fitzgerald's answers were not vague enough. The Committee came away with the impression that the cost overruns were enormous.

Consequently, he experienced a slow death at the Pentagon. He was harassed, excluded from meetings, denied access to important documents, and given busywork to do. His private life was investigated, his mail was opened, he was routinely demoted (the last demotion was being assigned to audit the military bowling alley in Thailand), and then, within a year after his testimony, was fired. Being up against the ever-powerful military-industrial complex, he could no longer get a job in the aerospace industry either.

So he sued to get his Air Force job back. While awaiting the verdict on his job, Fitzgerald delivered lectures, wrote an account of his Pentagon experience, *The High Priests of Waste,* and did consulting work for Senator Proxmire's Joint Economic Committee. His remarkable tenacity was in part due to his spontaneous sense of humor and his ability to "let go." With an Alabama drawl he remarked, "I used to say I was the only bureaucrat in the world suing for more work."

As word of his firing got out, his advice was sought by those who wanted a strong defense without bleeding taxpayers and who were frustrated by the lack of media follow-up on those concerns.

In 1973, after four years of legal battles, the Civil Service Commission ordered his reinstatement. Nevertheless, the Air Force persisted in denying him access to important materials dealing with major weapons purchases, and consigned him to largely meaningless paperwork.

In 1974, he sued again. Thirteen years after his first lawsuit, he was awarded $200,000 in legal fees and obtained a federal court order requiring the Air Force to give him a job with duties equal to those he had previously. As a result of later negotiations, he was paid $142,000 by former President Richard Nixon. Nixon, as was revealed by the White House tapes during the Watergate investigation, had personally ordered that Fitzgerald be fired.

After his reinstatement, Fitzgerald found that the cost-overrun abuses had actually increased. He calculated that some contractors were so inefficient that they would have to charge $100,000 for a tv set that would normally sell for $400 in the commercial market.

Fitzgerald's civil service rating placed him at the same level as a three-star general. However, the Air Force interfered with his access to records. Staff generals insisted that his requests first meet their approval despite the court order. He was denied information from lower-ranking military officials and experienced delays in filing requests until the material was too late to have impact.

In 1984, the Air Force waited until the last minute before refusing Fitzgerald permission to testify in his "official" capacity to the Senate Government Affairs Committee about Pentagon purchasing and auditing practices. His superior suggested that he retestify as a "private citizen." Fitzgerald, however, refused to weaken his whistle-blowing rights by testifying unofficially. The stalemate continued until Senator Charles Grassley arranged hearings on information-access problems for the Judiciary Subcommittee on Administrative Practice and Procedure.

The Air Force once again pulled rank at the last minute, forcing Fitzgerald to cancel his testimony. By then, Senator Grassley was so irate that he obtained a subpoena and, accompanied by tv crews, *hand*-delivered the summons to Fitzgerald at the Pentagon—a pattern which Senator Grassley has repeated since with a surprising degree of success.

In his testimony, Fitzgerald accused the Air Force of having withheld important information from him, thereby limiting his capability and authority. He continued to experience harassment, unfavorable job reviews, and bureaucratic busywork—all of which violated the 1982 court order that restored him to his job.

In spite of the sea of hostility constantly surrounding him, Fitzgerald continued to maintain a sense of humor, calling himself a "kindly gray-haired old gentleman." What whistle-blowers needed, he believed, was an objective, independent organization that would process its information and get it to the right sources.

That's when he called on Dina Rasor.

IV. Dina Rasor

Born in Los Angeles, Dina Rasor graduated from the University of California at Berkeley with a major in political science and a minor in journalism. Eager to enter the field of investigative journalism in national politics, and bound and determined not to have to pay her ten-year dues at a "podunk" newspaper, Rasor headed straight for Washington, D.C. She took a job as editorial assistant at ABC Radio News, and took on a brief documentary project for the President's Commission on Coal before accepting a job at the National Taxpayer's Union (NTU). Her assignment was to investigate waste and fraud in government programs, write articles for the NTU newsletter, and prepare testimony.

While following up on a Lockheed C-5A wing fix scandal in 1980, she came across Fitzgerald's name. She discovered that Fitzgerald had been chairman of the NTU and a major force in the taxpayer movement for many years until he regained his job at the Air Force.

Fitzgerald turned out to be both her guide and mentor. Expecting to meet an embittered man, she found him to be a determined optimist who believed the misspending, waste, and fraud could be eliminated. From his thirty-year experience, she gained insights into the Pentagon system of monitoring procurement. She learned that purchasing abuses were common to all branches of the military. He helped her develop techniques for communicating technical information to the public. He encouraged her to maintain her personal integrity no matter how great the pressure or provocation. She discovered it was easier to make decisions when she knew she didn't have to compromise. She relished the investigation of the C-5A wing fix for the NTU and wanted more opportunities for defense investigation. In the course of her research, she adopted a personal cause on behalf of the servicemen who were needlessly killed by malfunctioning or inadequate equipment.

Fitzgerald was impressed with her clear perceptions of military documents. Her articles were written from the viewpoint of both taxpayers and servicemen. Cognizant of Rasor's growing frustration over the fact that Pentagon waste and fraud issues were becoming increasingly difficult to pursue at NTU, Fitzgerald suggested that she start her own organization to serve as a front for "closet patriots" inside the Pentagon. With such protection, military excesses could be exposed to the public while keeping whistle-blowers anonymous and enabling them to continue to ferret out internal information. This way attention could be deflected from the whistle-blowers to the offending bureaucrats. The public could pressure Congress and the Department of Defense to get the best weapons at the best price.

Fitzgerald's proposal seemed almost overwhelming at first to the twenty-four-year-old journalist. Rasor could hardly imagine that she was qualified to start her own organization. Nevertheless, she was exhilarated by the possibility. She figured that she could get by with office space large enough for a desk and a phone. She had a few press contacts from previous NTU investigations. She would take on one weapons project at a time. She arranged to continue working only parttime at NTU to allow herself time to find funding, with some good leads from Fitzgerald. The Project for Military Procurement was established in 1981.

A process quickly emerged. Rasor digested and translated esoteric information from "closet patriots" and then passed along this information to responsible and effective journalists known for their follow-through on defense-related matters. She was getting results, and the project's business flourished. Like CDI, the project's success was especially noteworthy in light of its prohibition against using classified information. Rasor felt that the strongest cases were made with the Department of Defense's own documentation.

She called her network of informants the "Pentagon Underground." The Project served to unify all the underground members —the majority of whom included scientists and weapons designers; former and current military officers and enlisted personnel; cost analysts and auditors—into a single purpose: to buy more effective weapons at a lower cost.

Another element of success was that Rasor chose to focus on the cost-effectiveness of weapons, remaining detached from foreign policy ideology. This is what she had promised the underground and what enabled her to tap a wide variety of sources. She had seen both anti- and pro-military groups be discredited by taxpayers on their foreign policy recommendations.

Rasor's first investigative effort was the Army's continuing M-1 tank production in spite of two sets of unacceptable test results. She quickly discovered the many ways that faulty weapons are "justified" by the Pentagon bureaucracy in order to sustain the flow of money to the contractors. The military establishment either ignores the results, rigs the tests, or, as she personally experienced, sends out "abridged" test reports. Her Congressional testimony on the M-1 tank won her a Senatorial invitation to operate an M-1 tank and compare it to the M-60, an older model. She had prepared herself so thoroughly on the subject of tanks that she was able to confirm the complaints of the soldiers who had used the tanks in battle conditions.

The biggest breakthrough for the Project's credibility with the press came with the release of results of OTIII (operational test number three) on the M-1 tank, which were bad and in some respects worse than the previous OTs I and II. The Project juxtaposed the Army's claims and Congressional testimony with actual test results. The discrepancies couldn't have been more obvious. All the major newspapers carried the story.

Journalists with little technical knowledge of defense and limited access to information are sometimes reluctant to tackle a weapons-procurement story. The Project, therefore, provides defense reporters with *relevant* facts on Pentagon waste. It helps journalists and congressmen to recognize the flaws in Pentagon handouts and how to evaluate actual weapon effectiveness in the context of intended use. It serves as a memory bank for Congress on Pentagon promises and deliveries. It offers protection to whistle-blowers who provide evidence of waste and fraud. The Project has also assisted congressmen in drafting legislation to improve weapons procurement practices. An example would be the separation of operational testing of weapons from weapons developers. The Project also exerts pressure on the Department of Defense to carry out legislated reforms.

By early 1983, the Project was beginning to see the fruits of its labor. Some influential conservatives were becoming convinced that the Pentagon spending spree was hurting both the American military and the economy. A couple of years later, a general audience had evolved as well. The public was becoming increasingly alert to Pentagon waste; it recognized that military spending did not necessarily guarantee greater national security.

Grassley, La Rocque, Fitzgerald, and Rasor have demonstrated that, as adept and powerful as the bureaucracy has become at obtaining large sums for weapons programs, it is not beyond public reach and correction.

* * *

At the American Constitutional Convention in Philadelphia, Madison and Hamilton argued that government could be no better than its defined structure, which the Constitution sought to provide. They believed good men would find it difficult to function, let alone come to the top, in poorly structured government; and that bad men would misuse the power that such a structure made possible. They put their emphasis on structure and law, which is to say, a system of balanced and responsible powers. They understood the tendency of a strong military presence, with its exemptions, loopholes, and administrative decisions, to weaken the structure of democratic government.

The economic implications of these facts are readily recognizable. High employment, for example, is an imperative in American society, or any society for that matter. Conversely, high unemployment is an economic blight and a source of political unrest. The ability of the Defense Department to enlist American labor unions, along with industry, in the campaign for maximum military budgets has become an important part of the way political power is being used for Pentagon programs.

The alliance of labor and industry has been especially potent in the Congress. Hardly a state in the Union has not received military contracts or has not been a beneficiary, directly or indirectly, of military programs. Members of Congress quickly get the message that their chances of keeping their seats are connected to their ability to get a full share of military spending for their own states and districts. The higher the total appropriations, the greater the probability of high local distribution. Political campaign contributions in many cases are almost in direct proportion to the ability of members of Congress to vote for Pentagon requests.

The extension of military power into politics is not new, nor is it limited to the elective process. It extends into every function of government, including the making of foreign policy. At one time, the role of the military was strictly confined to carrying out the decisions of civilian policy makers. But the growth in military spending, especially in recent years, has given military authorities a significant place in the policy-making councils of government. Just as the State Department has its embassies and consulates around the world, so the Defense Department has maintained hundreds of stations abroad for intelligence and influence purposes. Not infrequently, military rather than diplomatic officials have represented the U.S. government abroad on sensitive and significant issues.

In response to public outrage over government and media reports of procurement extravagance within the defense industry, President Reagan, in July 1985, appointed a blue-ribbon commission, headed by former Deputy Secretary of Defense David Packard

(Chief Executive Officer of Hewlett-Packard, a major defense contractor), to investigate defense management practices. In its February 1986 interim report, the Commission recommended changes in both procedures and personnel in order to upgrade the quality, usefulness, and efficiency of weapons programs while minimizing wastefulness and cost. Some of those recommendations included the making of provisional five-year defense budgets and two-year defense appropriations, the creation of an Undersecretary of Defense for Acquisitions, a consolidation of all federal procurement statutes into a single, consistent, and simplified government-wide procurement statute, the use of more "off-the-shelf" rather than "custommade" products and services, and the encouragement of commercial-style competition in weapons programs.

The Commission put its emphasis on the need for defense contractors to follow a self-determined code of ethics, rather than on the criminal prosecution of offenders. It did, however, in its June 1986 report to the President, recommend that Federal Acquisition Regulations should specify precise criteria for determining contractor responsibility. These recommendations could have been usefully applied the previous year. In 1985, following investigations for fraud, General Dynamics was "reprimanded" with a brief suspension of its contracts with the Navy. Moreover, the Navy assured the company it would not sever its relations with it. (A fuller account of the General Dynamics investigation is presented in a later, separate chapter.)

With each turn of the scientific wheel, with its new weapons or systems, the argument is advanced that we are on the threshold of a great advantage. But the advantage quickly is transformed into an additional threat when the other side, inevitably, finds a way of duplicating those weapons or counteracting them, thus giving substance to one of history's oldest lessons: namely, that two nations of approximately the same power can set the stage for mutual annihilation.

8

The Gold-Tipped Iceberg

D eep beneath the surface of things are markers betraying the presence of veritable icebergs of overcharge and waste.

The $7,600 coffee maker or the $15,000 couch are not glitches but indicators pointing to other products of mismanagement and sometimes fraud, whose cost to the taxpayer runs into billions of dollars.

The Committee on Armed Services of the House of Representatives has issued a report on the way the arms contractors took advantage of the taxpayers, passing along bills that had nothing to do with the national defense. For example, the report revealed that General Dynamics charged the government $1.4 million for trips taken by the executives in company jet planes. GD Chairman David S. Lewis, who received a yearly salary of $1,000,000, charged the government $320,000 for his frequent company plane trips from company headquarters in Clayton, Missouri, to his country home in Georgia. GD maintained an office in the nation's capital for the purpose of "legislation liaison," a euphemism for lobbying in behalf of its interests. This expense, amounting to $1.2 million, was billed to the taxpayers. Another item turned up by the House Armed Services Committee involved a request by a GD executive for reimbursement for attending 562 business conferences in a single year.

From 1978 to 1983, GD billed the government for $22 million in company plane expenses in transporting executives to ski resorts and sundry other places. Other charges that were supposedly in the interests of national security included $18,650 in initiation fees at a country club for a GD official, dues at the Washington, D.C., Burning Tree Country Club, payments to baby sitters, and kennel fees.

It must not be assumed that General Dynamics was the only arms contractor engaged in dishonest billing to the United States government. McDonnell-Douglas passed along to the government its public relations costs for attempting to enhance its image after the crash of a DC-10 in Chicago in 1979. Sperry Rand tried to get the government to pay $177,222 for its expenses in labor relations.

A number of contractors submitted bills amounting to $7,900,-000 for their exhibits at an air show in Paris. Though these exhibits were of benefit only to the companies and had little or no connection with military ordnance, the U.S. Treasury was asked to pay the costs of the exhibitions. For example, North American sent in a bill for $144,989 to pay for "display models." Boeing Aerospace passed along bills to the government amounting to $54,000 in travel costs associated with the Paris Air Show and $105 in traffic violations. Sperry charged the government $91,819 for advertising, even though advertising costs had been expressly disallowed. Convair attempted to get the government to pay $217,025 for emblems, souvenirs, models, and displays identifying Convair products.

Other items turned up by the House Committee investigators:

• Boeing charged the U.S. taxpayers $11,750 for its sponsorship of the World Paper Airplane Championship.

• Boeing passed along charges totaling $2,485 for golf fees, cart rentals, and liquor at executive meetings in Carlsbad, California, in April 1979 and Tucson, Arizona, in November 1979.

• General Dynamics passed along to the government its costs in attempting to sell its weapons to foreign countries.

• Rockwell charged the government for its executive dining room and cafeteria operations in the amount of $1,040,588.

• The Fort Worth division of General Dynamics sent in a bill for $10,713 to cover the losses of the company barber shop.

• Sperry tried to charge the government $160,480 for expenses incurred in connection with the sale of the company's commercial products in Europe.

  • Newport News sought reimbursement for a company house used almost exclusively by the president of the company.

  • McDonnell Aircraft claimed $1,558,377 for "rearrangement expenses," by which was meant a wide range of costs.

  • Sperry billed the government $899,982 for "traffic department" expenses.

In all, government auditors disallowed $110 million in bills passed along to the taxpayers. House Committee officials were criticized because this amount was only a small percentage of approved costs. To which the House officials replied:

All defense contractors are aware of the cost principles which are written into every contract and spelled out in Federal procurement regulations. Nevertheless, all too often contractors "get creative" in allocating and accumulating costs. For example, "entertainment" becomes "public relations" and "air shows" become "selling expenses" . . . it is clearly impossible for the Government's auditors to review each item in the company submission. We do not know . . . what percent of the total submission of any particular contractor has been subject to audit. At best, it is a relatively small portion of the indirect costs submitted.

Since company officials know that the entire submission will not be audited, there is little incentive for not submitting a cost element. The larger the submission, the more costs are incurred, be they unallowable, gray, or allowable, the greater the profits to the company if the costs are not challenged by the auditor. There are no penalties and even if the item is disallowed, it costs the company nothing. The burden of proof rests squarely on the Government . . . Information gathered in our review demonstrates that even when questioned, the seven companies were reimbursed for about 37 percent of the questioned costs . . . these results clearly show how advantageous it is for the defense contractors to amass as large a charge as possible for submission to the Government.

Far more significant and costly, of course, than the cheating on "expenses" were mistakes in judgment, mismanagement, and sometimes fraud, whose cost to the taxpayers ran into millions of dollars.

Like any organization, the Pentagon has taken pains to shield its blunders from public view. But in mid-1985, Secretary of Defense Caspar Weinberger publicly acknowledged that the Sergeant York Weapons system, otherwise called DIVAD, for "Division Air Defense," had been a mistake. (Since military terminology is a blood relative of police-blotter English, it should be mentioned here that "weapons system" is Pentagonese for a plane, a tank, a fighting ship, or—in the case of the Sergeant York—an anti-aircraft gun.)

Speaking of the Sergeant York in somber measures, Secretary Weinberger explained that, in spite of its long development and testing ($1.8 billion worth), it would now be discontinued. On paper, the Sergeant York was a dream weapon: a highly mobile, tanklike land dreadnought armed with two ugly-looking antiaircraft cannon guided by radar and computers. The idea was that the radar scanner would pick up incoming enemy aircraft trying to attack our tank columns. Computers would then aim the cannon. All the gunner had to do was squeeze the trigger (a flashing FIRE NOW sign would even tell the the gunner when!). The Sergeant York fairly bristled with such "bells and whistles" (Pentagonese for costly gadgets).

Unfortunately, on the testing grounds the Sergeant York's radar gear proved incapable of picking up fast-moving fighter planes—it was, in fact, blind even to bulky helicopters hanging still in midair. Another problem: the "all-weather" attack planes the Sergeant York was designed to defend our tank divisions against don't, in fact, work too well in cloudy weather, which fouls up their radar gun-aiming gear. So these all-weather craft are sent up only in ideal weather. Even in clear daylight, the radar-equipped state-of-the-art F-15E attack plane (cost: $40 million each) is not accurate within 100 feet when it is bombing tanks.

When it thus became clear that the Sergeant York was a fancy but ineffective cannon with a severe shortage of enemy planes to shoot at, the military abruptly shifted its ground. The Sergeant York was now needed, they said, to shoot down helicopter gunships. But the trouble with this notion was that Vietnam had long since proved that helicopters are highly vulnerable to ordinary, inexpensive light weapons. In Vietnam, Vietcong rifle and machine-gun fire had brought thousands of expensive copters fluttering or crashing to earth. Why, then, build a radar-guided cannon to do what light weapons, including rifles and machine guns, were already doing better? (The wholesale downing of helicopters in Vietnam was no fluke. The Soviet Hind-D combat helicopter has proved equally vulnerable to rebel ground fire in Afghanistan.)

The Sergeant York's only shining hour came in 1980 with modest success against radio-controlled planes and helicopters. Some observers, however, were rude enough to point out that the downed targets had been maneuvered at constant speeds along flight paths straight as a string. This meant that even ordinary guns aimed by the eye would have been effective. Also, in battle action, fighter pilots go in for "evasive maneuvers"—they make their planes wriggle and "jink," that is, make sharp, erratic swerves from side to side. Further, during hot action even helicopters don't just hang in midair, motionless, waiting for enemy gunners below to zero in on them. But in the Pentagon's "test" of the Sergeant York, the target whirlybirds *were made to hover in place.* Even so, the gun's accuracy was spotty.

To compound the fiasco, the Sergeant York was constantly plagued by "down time" problems with its radar and other fragile electronics gear. It also had a nasty way of conking out in cold weather; it often stalled on semi-steep grades; and its twin cannon not only malfunctioned often but had a firing range of only about two and a half miles. This meant that missile-firing aircraft could stand well beyond the Sergeant York's range and shoot it at will. If the enemy missile was an infrared "heat seeker" it certainly couldn't miss: The Sergeant York's power system poured out so much heat that heat-seeking missiles found it a splendid "beacon" to home in on.

But if the Sergeant York was as flawed in this and later tests, how did it manage to shoot down any target planes at all? The shameful truth is that, as the *New York Times* recorded in an article on August 29, 1985, the Sergeant York's "testers" resorted to rigged testing. As is standard, the pilotless radio-controlled target planes were routinely equipped with explosive "safety" charges, so they could be blown up if anything went wrong. To make the Sergeant

York look deadly accurate the friendly testers merely waited for several seconds after it was fired, then detonated the target plane's safety charges by remote control! As fiery fragments of the plane fluttered to earth, the Army tester would calmly score its destruction as a "hit" for the Sergeant York.

Despite the Sergeant York's scandalously inept performances, which were an open secret even to non-Pentagon observers, the military kept pushing its pet project right up to the day, August 28, 1985, when Secretary Weinberger cancelled it.

And what of the $3 billion "saved" by phasing out this over-engineered specimen? The Pentagon has made it clear that these monies would be used to "identify" and develop a new anti-aircraft gun that would do what the Sergeant York could not.

A footnote on the Sergeant York: Not since the late 1960s had a weapons system been dropped after getting so far along on the production line. The decision to put the gun into production despite its long record of abject failure in tests was a flagrant example of waste in the Pentagon.

The Sergeant York is not the only embarrassing failure in the Pentagon's stable of costly weapons.

The Airborne Dinosaur

Begin with the AH-64A Apache attack helicopter, pride of the Army's 9,000-copter "sky cavalry." Each helicopter costs $17 million. Bristling with laser-guided Hellcat missiles, this device has been presented to the public as a flying hedgehog, a weapons system that will sweep all before it by "vertically enveloping" enemy forces. Yet experience teaches—and Pentagon insiders privately admit—that helicopters, the AH-64 very much included, are death traps, pure and simple.

Early in the Vietnam War, Pentagon observers were appalled to find that their much-touted "flying tanks" were being crippled—in some cases blown apart while aloft—by weapons wielded by enemy foot soldiers. It was not a question of lucky hits on vulnerable spots; helicopters are not terribly stable. Heavy hits almost anywhere on the craft are likely to cause crashes. The Army admits that 4,900 whirlybirds were shot down in Vietnam—almost all by ground fire.

But here, as with the Sergeant York tests, creative bookkeeping seems to have been the order of the day. If friendly forces could retrieve the tail of a crashed copter complete with its service number, the tail would be sent back to the U.S. posthaste. There, a new copter would then be built, incorporating the old tail. The original crashed ship was thus considered "repaired," and never listed as a wipeout! It is believed that the actual number of helicopters destroyed in Vietnam was nearer 10,000 than the nearly 5,000 officially admitted.

In pondering these figures, keep in mind that, overwhelmingly, the vaunted helicopters or "flying tanks" lost in Vietnam were downed *by simple rifle and machine-gun fire.* The enemy had no air force to speak of, nor modern anti-aircraft batteries. There is something approaching the absurd about large numbers of AH-64s hovering over European-style battlefields. There they would be facing swarms of infinitely faster fighting jets, coming at them with rapid-fire cannon and laser-guided or heat-seeking missiles. Meanwhile, mobile anti-aircraft units, tank cannon, and small, bazooka-like missiles fired from the shoulders of infantrymen would be coming up at them from the ground. But wouldn't the AH-64 bob and weave, evasively? No: In order to line up its laser-guided missiles and launch them accurately, the AH-64 must hover in place invitingly for a good half minute! And in any case, helicopters aren't much good at jinking. They are far too slow and cumbersome to match jets at that game.

Despite these facts, the Army, for reasons that will follow, continued to push ahead with an unprecedented helicopter buildup, with the AH-64 as its centerpiece. And just as steadily, the price of the AH-64 has risen. In 1981, the glamour copter cost $9 million per copy. By 1983, the price had jumped to $17 million per unit.

If the AH-64 is clumsy, slow-moving, hard to maneuver, and not nearly so good at tank-killing as much less expensive jet fighters, why didn't the Army just order up jets, not helicopters, to blow enemy tanks apart? The answer lies in the bizarre compartmentalization of our armed forces that accounts for much of the Pentagon's inter-service myopia.

Civil War in Our Armed Forces

The U.S. Army, Navy, and Air Force have competed strenuously with one another for what each regards as its fair share of the military budget. The insularity of these services and their bitterness toward each other may seem incredible to ordinary citizens. But it is a fact of military life in the U.S.

By the late 1950s, the Air Force had pretty well convinced Congress that future wars would be fought high in the stratosphere with intercontinental ballistic missiles and bombers longer than a football field. The Air Force scored its gaudiest victory when, in 1957, it was given exclusive control of *all* fixed-wing aircraft weighing more than 5,000 pounds.

The Army interpreted this decision as meaning that it could have all the tiny Piper Cubs it wanted for artillery spotting and ferrying officers. But the once-mighty Army would now have to come to the Air Force whenever it needed fighting planes for "close support" actions—that is, firefights in which low-flying planes support ground troops by strafing, bombing, and generally harassing enemy troops. The Air Force, however, preoccupied with its grand vision of Armageddon at 100,000 feet, made it bitingly clear that it was not enamored with the notion of providing low-level close support for "grunts" and groundlings.

What to do? Rotary-wing aircraft didn't come under the fixed-wing ban. Why couldn't the Army use *helicopters* as the backbone of its close-support maneuvers?

Thus was born, out of necessity, the "sky cavalry" fighting-helicopter concept. Just as the sculptor Pygmalion fell in love with his own statue Galatea, so the Army soon fell in love with its new fighting helicopters. So did the movies, in which, deus ex machina-style, clusters of air-cavalry whirlybirds were shown descending on the battlefield in the nick of time (often to the strains of symphonic music). The public can be forgiven if it mistakenly places the helicopter on a par with the jet fighter as an engine of destruction.

Despite the wretched record of fighting helicopters in Vietnam, the Iran-Iraq war, and the Soviet intervention in Afghanistan, the Army continued to press for more AH-64A choppers at $17 million a copy. Procurement costs for the program already exceed a total of $6.5 billion. Though expert opinion holds that helicopters can transport the wounded and supplies, no one can justify their existence as fighting machines.

AWACS: The High-Tech Supersnooper

While the Army was building up the supply of Sergeant York guns and attack helicopters, the Air Force was all aglow over its new spy plane, called the Advanced Warning and Control System (AWACS). This was not, Air Force spokesmen said, just a plane; it was an aerial command post in an age of "electronic battlefield" wars. Bristling with arcane radar and electronic gear, AWACS was designed to monitor both air and ground space for hundreds of miles around. Its snooping equipment was said to be able to pick up conversations on the ground, far below, and its radar could spot low-flying enemy aircraft hundreds of miles away. Further, AWACS could even direct large numbers of fighter bombers, guiding them unerringly to their targets.

Starry-eyed over this prospect, the Air Force signed up for thirty-five of the superplanes, at a cost of $9 billion, although some observers predicted that the actual cost would come to twice that amount. Still, costs seemed secondary in buying a plane that might win World War III.

It wasn't long, however, before AWACS's reputation began to shred. In tests over Europe, the plane's radar shocked Air Force personnel by "seeing" hundreds of low-flying unidentified aircraft moving about in the skies below. It turned out that these "planes" were cars driving along a highway near Frankfurt, West Germany. Then, during a May 1975 test, specialists aboard a Navy EA-6B "Prowler" plane unlimbered a device that effectively jammed the radar images received by an AWACS plane 350 miles away. The AWACS was thus rendered blind. To make things worse, the jamming device had been constructed from plans found in a Soviet textbook! While the AWACS radar was blacked out, two "enemy" planes were able to get within fifty yards of the "super-snooper" *without being spotted.* (These facts came to light when in June 1975 Senator Tom Eagleton asked the General Accounting Office to give him a report on the incident.)

Further investigation showed that AWACS's much-touted electronic armamentarium is "down" more than it is up: A 1979 test showed the gear was battle-ready only 15 percent of the time. When test standards were obligingly lowered, the "in-service" percentage rose to only 54 percent of the time. Richard Allen, President Reagan's first assistant for national security affairs, acknowledged in 1981 that AWACS break down so often the country would have to have five of them on the ground for every one that was aloft.

American taxpayers have paid billions of dollars for a military system that is quirky, over-engineered, and not up to the glittering claims the Pentagon has made for it.

The Mobile Crematorium

When the Bradley M-2 Infantry Fighting Vehicle was proclaimed by the military in the late 1970s, America's foot soldiers must have rejoiced. For here at last was a battlefield taxi that would speed infantrymen to the fighting in style, racing right alongside the tanks. Further, the Bradley was described as a taxi with teeth: As the soldiers inside fired at the enemy through six gun ports, the vehicle's twin 25-mm cannon and its tank-killer guided missiles could blast away at enemy concentrations up to two miles away.

Accurate aiming of the cannon was made easy by the behemoth's "integrated sight unit" which could see through fog, smoke, or even leafy green camouflage. On paper, this hulking troop carrier was a one-vehicle revolution in ground fighting.

Dazzled by its potential, the Army pushed the Bradley Fighting Vehicle into production without testing it fully. The plan was to acquire 6,882 Bradleys at a cost of almost $2 million each, a total cost of $13.7 billion. But all too soon, flaws began to crop up. One of the Bradley's strong points was supposed to be that in emergencies it could be rolled right into a giant transport plane and whisked off to distant hot spots. But the designers had neglected to make the vehicle narrow enough to fit into the mammoth carriers. This meant that the Bradley's heavy, five-and-one-half-inch-thick armor had to be unbolted so the carrier could be pulled aboard the transport by winches. At the other end, when unloaded, the vehicle's armor would be bolted back on. In a situation where minutes count, this disassemble-assemble sequence chewed up more than two hours of valuable "rapid deployment" time.

Almost as troublesome as the Bradley's girth was its ten-foot height, which increased its vulnerability to enemy gunners. The Army had phased out its ten-foot-high M-10 tank on the grounds that it was "too tall"; yet it was apparently untroubled by the Bradley's height.

Though designed as a troop-carrying vehicle, the Bradley, it turned out, had room for three crewmen and only six soldiers—a mere half a squad. If one is to believe the manufacturers, these six soldiers were safe and secure because they were protected by five-and-one-half inches of rock-hard aluminum armor. But under the right conditions—namely, a square hit by a mortar shell, a land mine, or even the right kind of grenade—this aluminum armor might ignite and burn fiercely, incinerating the occupants. The thicker such armor, the more intense and devastating the conflagration it would fuel. If the vehicle's commander tried to stave off attack by firing his guided missiles, he had a problem: The carrier must lurch to a dead stop if the missile were to be fired accurately. During that time the Bradley is a sitting duck—especially for the $150, shoulder-fired rockets now in existence in other countries.

According to William Boly, writing in *California Magazine* for February 1983, David Stockman, then the Reagan administration's budget director, had proposed that the Bradley be phased out. The request was denied. Reporter Boly also describes a field test he attended at which the Bradley's highly touted TOW guided missile fell far short of its target, and its machine guns jammed. Boly's conclusion: The Bradley Fighting Vehicle—named for the distinguished World War II General Omar Bradley—is a $13.7 billion dud.

The M-16: A Rifle That Couldn't

The most telling assessment of the M-16 rifle—the shoulder weapon issued to American foot soldiers in Vietnam—was made, mutely, by the enemy. When the Vietcong won a firefight, they would pick the dead clean of everything useful—boots, canteens, knives, grenades, rations, and so on. Even relatively outmoded rifles of World War II vintage were eagerly snatched up. Yet the Vietcong disdained the M-16s, leaving them behind on the ground.

In a notable article on the M-16 in *The Atlantic Monthly* for June 1981, James Fallows quotes from various letters sent home by American foot soldiers in Vietnam:

"Our M-16s aren't worth much . . . Out of 40 rounds I've fired, my rifle jammed about 10 times . . . These rifles are getting a lot of guys killed because they jam so easily . . ." "The weapon has failed us at crucial moments . . . as many as 50 percent of the rifles fail to work." "During this fight . . . I lost some of my best buddies. I personally checked their weapons. Close to 70 percent had a round stuck in the chamber, and take my word it was not their fault."

These cries from the heart might ordinarily be brushed aside by the military as "merely anecdotal." But as it happens, at least one

Congressional inquiry and at least one Army field test—at Fort Ord, in 1965—have clearly underlined the truth of these "anecdotal" criticisms.

The waste implicit in such wars-of-the-future systems as the Sergeant York can be measured by the billions of dollars they have chewed up. But how to measure the "cost" of the deaths in Vietnam traceable to the M-16's chronic malfunctioning?

How could the M-16 debacle have occurred? The long road to the M-16 began with the M-14 rifle, a postwar weapon that could fire its .30-caliber bullets either semi-automatically (a separate trigger squeeze for each bullet fired) or automatically (a steady stream of bullets is fired as long as the trigger is kept squeezed). Unfortunately, during automatic fire the M-14 bucked and jolted so violently that it was hard to aim.

The Army's solution to this problem was the AR-15 rifle, invented by weapons designer Eugene Stoner and made by the Armalite Corporation. Because it fired high-impact .22-caliber bullets, the AR-15 was much lighter than the M-14. This meant each soldier could carry three times as many bullets and keep firing that much longer. Further, since it had minimal "kick" or recoil, the rifle was easily aimed even when it was spurting out 600 bullets a minute. And —a crucial point—the AR-15 was virtually jam-proof. In all, it seemed that America's infantrymen were about to be issued a dream weapon.

As things turned out, the Green Berets and the paratroopers requested and got AR-15s. But in the early 1960s the Army Materiel Command, after elaborate tests, blocked the AR-15's general issuance. The rifle, said the Material Command's ordnance people, was inferior to the older M-14 rifle. This pronouncement struck many people as fishy. When Secretary of the Army Cyrus Vance later checked out the ordnance tests, he made a strange discovery: The tests had been tilted in favor of the M-14! (The details are vividly laid out in James Fallows's *Atlantic Monthly* article, mentioned above.)

There were rumblings about the Army ordnance experts being miffed because they had been bypassed in favor of an outside person, Eugene Stoner, and because Olin Mathieson and other companies that ordnance traditionally dealt with had been bypassed in favor of an "outside" company, Armalite. In any case, it seemed clear that for whatever reason, someone high up had it in for the AR-15.

Without consulting designer Stoner, the ordnance people set out to "improve" the AR-15 by festooning it with "bells and whistles." Among other modifications, they arbitrarily changed the type of gunpowder used in the ammunition and introduced a new pattern of spiral grooving in the gun's barrel. The result was a strangely transmogrified A-15 rifle, now dubbed the M-16.

As the soldiers' letters quoted earlier attest, this "bells and whistles" version jammed disastrously both in tests and on the battlefields (partly because the new powder—made by Olin Mathieson—"burned dirty" and fouled the mechanism). The bullets it fired lacked the impact and killing power of those fired from AR-15s; and the rate of fire, now raised to a risky 1,000 rounds a minute, brought on overheating and malfunction.

When the House Armed Services Committee investigated the M-16 situation in 1967, it found that although tests had repeatedly established the weapon's unreliability—especially when the new powder was used—the weapon nonetheless ended up on the Vietnam battlefields. The subcommittee reported concluded that "The failure . . . of officials with authority in the Army to . . . correct the deficiencies of the 5.56-mm ammunition borders on criminal negligence."

The C-5 Transport Plane

The saga of the C-5 transport plane is reminiscent of a prime-time soap opera in which the banished family black sheep keeps turning up under a new name.

Our story dates from the late 1950s, when the Air Force commissioned the Lockheed Company to build a giant, long-range cargo plane that could scoop up troops, artillery, and vehicles at a moment's notice and whisk them off to distant hot spots. The plane, called the C-5 (later the C-5A Galaxy), was truly a monster, as was its price tag. The Galaxy was the biggest plane in the sky.

But soon after the giant plane's introduction, Air Force operations people began protesting that the C-5 was all wrong for the job it was supposed to do. Instead of setting down on small landing strips close by raging battles, so as to disgorge urgently needed supplies and fighting men, this aerial brontosaurus required king-sized concrete runways of the sort found only at major airports and military bases far from battlefronts. Even on the few military bases that could accommodate it, the C-5 was so big that there were few places to park it for needed servicing between flights.

By the late 1960s the C-5 had accumulated a record cost overrun of $2 billion in excess of its original cost estimate. Worse, it was developing ugly cracks in the wings. Lockheed's solution? It asked the government for $1.5 billion to set the wings right! This was too much even for the Pentagon, and the C-5 program was finally shut down in the early 1970s.

With the 1980s came renewed support for the "rapid deployment" concept—the tactic of airlifting troops and supplies to the scene of distant fighting. Two big defense contractors, McDonnell-Douglas and Boeing, submitted designs for the needed plane, and in 1981 McDonnell-Douglas was told by the Pentagon that its C-17 design had won out. A few days later, Lockheed, belatedly and brazenly, disinterred its C-5 design, added a few changes, called the "new" plane the C-5B, and asked the Pentagon to reverse its decision.

Predictably, many Air Force people were outraged. The C-5, they protested, was three times as expensive to maintain as the C-17, gobbled up far more spare parts, and was a whale out of water when trying to land on air strips anywhere near putative battle fields. The Army, Air Force, and Marine Corps chiefs wrote to Congress in November 1981 strongly backing the C-17. In January 1982, the secretary of the Air Force sharply criticized the C-5 and affirmed the C-17's superiority. Such outright denunciations of a major weapons system had seldom been heard in Pentagon circles, and veteran reporters assumed that son-of-C-5 was a dead issue.

But within the month, Secretary of Defense Caspar Weinberger rejected the anti-C-5 statements and opted for Lockheed's C-5B system. Why? The answer highlights some of the realities about Defense Department procurement policies. Lockheed, the insiders said, had claimed that it was in deep financial trouble, so the Defense Department had decided to bail it out by giving the firm the lucrative contract. Its motive: to keep a key defense contractor strong in case we had to go to war. Swallowing hard, the anti-C-5B contingent in the military went along with the decision. Lockheed had brought off the neatest end run in procurement history. The C-5B program, it was estimated, would produce fifty planes and cost almost $11 billion.

And what of Boeing and McDonnell-Douglas, which had campaigned so hard for their clearly superior entries? Veteran observers believed that these companies had been assured it would all be made up to them in some future, similar situation.

Stealth Bombers: Ghosts in the Night Sky

The very phrase "stealth bomber" makes the back of one's neck prickle slightly: Invisible to radar, night bombers carrying nuclear weapons swoop undetected across enemy frontiers, and wreak unlimited destruction.

This chilling scenario was "leaked" rather noisily to the American public in 1980. But when pressed for details of the ghostly bombers they had gone out of their way to publicize, Pentagon spokesmen suddenly turned coy. Such matters, they intoned, are classified. This ploy proved irritating to experts outside the military because, they said, the evidence seemed to show that "stealth" techniques are all but useless. Even physicist Edward Teller, father of the H-bomb and a strong advocate of the "forward" stance in national security planning, voiced reservations about the extravagant claims made for stealth bombers. Teller warned of an easily deployed "countermeasure" the enemy could use to detect "stealth" overflights. But, walking on eggs, he refused to say more on grounds of secrecy.

Official protests to the contrary, there was good reason to suspect that the huge sums (one source speaks of $750 million a year) being spent on this "classified" program would go the way of monies expended on the Sergeant York gun and the C-5A transport plane.

As reporter Knut Royce made clear in several 1982 articles for the Hearst papers, the stealth idea derives from World War II. To foil Allied radar-detection devices being used against their submarines, German technologists coated the subs' snorkels with a layer of Teflon-like material that absorbed enemy radar waves instead of allowing them to bounce back to ships that had sent them out. This meant that the snorkels became, in effect, invisible.

Decades after the war, the Pentagon experimented with a small, high-speed "stealth" plane coated so as to absorb radar waves and become similarly invisible. By the 1980s, the Pentagon was going full blast on plans for a huge Stealth bomber. Pentagon people stiffened and clammed up when the bomber was mentioned by "outsiders," but a steady trickle of piquant details was somehow leaked to reporters—among them, the facts that the bomber would have rounded-off surfaces and would weigh a whopping 550,000 pounds (more than the gigantic B-52 bomber!).

Ordinarily, such an ambitious, expensive program would have had to win Congressional approval. But the Stealth project bypassed governmental scrutiny because it was paid for from the Pentagon's discretionary fund, known as their "black money."

If the Stealth program had not been secretly developed but instead had to justify itself to the Congress, what might have happened? Is it possible that the Congress would have concluded that *total* invisibility to radar is a daydream? A properly coated, properly contoured plane might get twice as close to a radar-protected target as an ordinary plane—but it could not escape radar altogether.

Size is crucial. The greater the approaching craft's size and girth, the easier it is for radar to pick it up. (The U-boats' coated snorkels were, of course, relatively slim.) The original stealth-plane proposal envisaged a small, probably needle-thin, 15,000-pound craft. But the enormous "stealth" bomber would be hard for radar *not* to pick up! According to impartial observers, the radar-foiling layer of coating needed for a bomber that big would have to be quite heavy, and *four feet thick.* This alone would severely diminish the plane's performance, especially on long-range missions.

Is it heresy for the mere layman to speculate on what a counter-measure might be? For decades, Air Force spokesmen have boasted of having heat-detector cameras and viewing instruments that enable night-flying planes to spot heat emissions from moving vehicles on the ground far below. In Vietnam, ground-level forces used such detectors to locate enemy troops. If enemy forces used similar de-vices to monitor the night skies near the borders, wouldn't they be able to spot the furnace-hot exhaust blasts given off by a 550,000-pound bomber passing overhead? Perhaps the Pentagon has found a way to keep giant planes from releasing heat into the air, but if so, they have not claimed credit for such an invention.

Experts contended that the Pentagon had undertaken a terrifi-cally costly program, paid for with public funds and immune from any accounting to the American Congress. Granted the occasional need for secrecy in the name of national security, it is important to ask whether public scrutiny has been resisted because of the legiti-mate requirements of security or because the officials involved wanted to insulate themselves from criticism.

9

Weapons Waste

A good way of scrutinizing military mismanagement of public funds is to consider other examples of decision making that result in flawed weapons systems. For example, the M-1 Abrams tank. The cost to the American taxpayer is $3 million per tank. Advertised to the public as the key weapon in our ground-assault forces, it actually serves as a prime exhibit of what some observers have called "wonder junk."

According to Pentagon publicity releases, the Chrysler-built Abrams tanks are encased in impenetrable Cobham "magic armor," and charge across the battlefield at fifty miles an hour. As the behemoths crunched across rough terrain, their four-man crews are supposed to be able to fire laser-guided cannon without having to slacken the tank's pace. One has a picture of the M-1 leaving a trail of blown-up enemy tanks behind them. With such spectacular victories in the offing, who could begrudge the roughly $20 billion the M-1 program would cost the U.S.?

But the evidence does not support the claims. The evidence indicates that the M-1 couldn't shoot straight; breaks down with appalling frequency; has armor penetrated by existing missiles and 125-mm cannon; and is too big to transport by ordinary means. When its cannon is elevated above a certain height, a gap appearsd between the turret and hull that makes the tank a ready target for enemy cannoneers. One critic pointed out that, considering the

M-1's frequent breakdowns, it may be one of the *slowest* tanks in the world, not the fastest.

Though all these defects have been documented since the M-1 program was begun in 1972, the Department of Defense has pushed many thousands of uncorrected M-1s into production. In the process, military officials have replaced the M-60, a reliable if less gussied-up tank which costs less than a million dollars—compared with the $3 million M-1. The Army has refused to test the M-1s against the M-60s, in a 3-to-1 cost ratio. The military's determination to field the patently flawed M-1 weapons system may be suggestive of the decision to equip our troops in Vietnam with the undependable M-16 rifle.

Those who know how solicitous U.S. Army officers are of the lives of their troops may wonder how the M-1 ever found its way to potential fighting fronts. Would the influence of the manufacturers be a clue?

The Backdrop

The M-1 tank program dates from November 1972. In the Armed Forces tradition of naming weapons after estimable military figures—e.g., the Sergeant York cannon and the (General Omar) Bradley troop carrier—the M-1 tank is called the Abrams, after Army Chief of Staff General Creighton Abrams.

The Abrams tank has a theoretical 50-mph road speed (most impressive for a hulking sixty-ton tank clanking along on treads), made possible by an aircraft-type 1500-horsepower gas turbine engine. The M-1's vaunted Cobham body armor, originated in England, is made up of layers of "super-alloy" metal and fiberglass. It is theoretically invulnerable to cannon shells.

When lurching and jouncing across battlefields, ordinary tanks must slam to a stop before firing their cannon, on pain of shooting wild. Not so the M-1: its 105-mm cannon is set into a turret so well stabilized that the gun is supposed to fire accurately on, so to speak, the dead run. If a fire breaks out inside the tank—a common hazard in these machines—an elaborate fire-control system is supposed to detect the flareup and snuff the fire out immediately. The gunner doesn't even have to sight through crude optical instruments to determine how far away oncoming targets are. An ultramodern laser range finder does the job for him. And if the battlefield is obscured by clouds of smoke and dust, or if night has fallen, the tank's heat-detecting apparatus can pierce the gloom and pick up heat waves given off by enemy tanks.

With its great speed and devastatingly accurate firepower, the M-1, according to the Pentagon, is "the Army's single most important weapon system . . . possibly into the next century."

In *More Bucks, Less Bang,* a study for the Project on Military Procurement, Dina Rasor cites a field test at Fort Knox in which three M-1s suffered mission-interrupting breakdowns every thirty-four miles during 16,070 miles on the road. Though the Army had thought the M-1 would have a cruising range of about 300 miles, Rasor cites Army tests showing that the M-1 is actually good for only 130 miles (its "inferior" predecessor, the doughty M-60, has a cruising range of 160 miles).

By Army standards, at least 50 percent of any given group of M-1s should be able to cruise for 4,000 miles without needing overhaul of their power trains—engine, transmission, and front drive. But at Fort Knox in 1980, only 22 percent of the M-1s tested met this standard. A year later, according to a congressional study, the figure had dropped to only 19 percent.

The "getting-there" picture darkened further as more test results came out. The M-1, Dina Rasor learned from these tests, was hypersensitive to the dust kicked up as tanks roll along in column formation. Once every eighty miles or so, the M-1's air filters clogged up, and a tank had to drop out of formation so the crew could clean up the filters or install new ones. The tank's treads were another vulnerable point: though designed to last for 2,000 miles, they broke down, on average, at 850 miles.

If the tank is so bad at getting to the arena of combat, why not load it onto a heavy truck or a train and transport it somewhere near the battle action? Not so simple. The M-1 is so huge and ungainly that only one of them can be loaded aboard the same railroad flatcars that easily handle *two* M-60s.

The On-Site Saga

Granted that the M-1 has problems getting there, doesn't it at least perform well once it arrives? Consider its most basic failure—its frequent inability to shoot straight. From time to time the NATO forces hold a kind of "tank Olympics," a grand shoot-out that is usually won by the German entries. In the June 1981 Olympics, the American entry was favored because it had the exotic laser and thermal-imaging devices used on the M-1. But the Germans won out even though their tank men used ordinary optical sighting devices. The Belgian team came in second, and the U.S. a dim third.

When the M-1 was later matched against a Belgian Leopold II tank and won the contest, the M-1's claque was jubilant. Then it turned out that the U.S. crew, distrustful of the M-1's bells and whistles, had disconnected the fancy turret stabilizer, had bypassed the fancy laser-thermal aiming apparatus, and had used their naked eyes to level in on the targets. (The turret stabilizers had been supplied with an "off" switch at the request of the crews!)

With or without the help of its automatic stabilizer, the M-1's swiveling turret is a headache: It juts out so far that land mines and grenade-throwing enemy soldiers in front of the tank cannot be spotted if they are less than twenty-seven feet away. Further, tank expert Robert J. Icks claims that when the M-1's cannon is raised for high-angle firing, as mentioned earlier, a dangerous gap opens up between the turret and the main body of the tank. Heavy machine gun fire directed into this opening could create mischief, and a heavy-duty hand grenade, a shell, or a missile, might blow the turret clear off.

Another problem: Infantrymen seeking shelter from enemy fire traditionally crouch close behind tanks as they advance across the battlefield. But the M-1's gas-turbine exhaust blasts make any such approach to the machine a flirtation with cremation. These same exhaust blasts make it unfeasible for one M-1 to hook onto another disabled M-1 and tow it off the battlefield for repairs.

It may be asked whether the M-1's tons of "magic" Cobham armor plating more than make up for the tank's various deficiencies. They might, if the armor really repelled shells and missiles. But it is an open secret among armor experts that 125-mm tank shells can slice through the much-touted Cobham armor.

The Army has attempted to deal with these disclosures by declaring that the armor's performance is a top-secret matter. This move was apparently aimed at eliminating independent scrutiny by American reporters. (The secrecy was hardly directed at the Soviets, who can easily enough obtain the armor for testing.)

Second, the military has quietly begun to plan ways of doing away with the offending turret—though they still maintain nothing is wrong with it. The attempt is to design a turretless mobile system that will do all that a turreted tank now does. Unfortunately, this design has been demonstrated to introduce a mare's nest of new problems. Experts have raised important questions: Now, for instance, will the crew, hunkered down inside the low hull, get a good 360-degree view of the battle action exploding all around them? Won't the turretless tank's ammunition supplies be smaller than the M-1's? These are only several of the headaches implicit in the projected design.

The Army's third, and main, way of dealing with the M-1's manifest deficiencies has been simply to express confidence in the tank. As reporters Patrick Oster and Bruce Ingersoll told the story in the *Chicago Sun-Times,* Army spokesmen simply bypassed the fact that foot soldiers cannot get protection by sticking close behind the M-1. Infantrymen, these spokesmen contended, have long since given up using tanks as shields, because tanks attract too much enemy fire.

What about the blind spot in front of the M-1? No matter, the Army explained: The tank is so formidable otherwise that the blind area is offset. As to the long list of other complaints, among them frequent breakdowns, Army spokesmen referred to the many "fixes" being planned: improved armor and bigger cannon among them. In effect, the Army spokesmen minimized the flaws but said they are spending millions of dollars to fix them!

One reason it is difficult to obtain definitive information about these flaws is that the tests, to say the least, are often incomplete. In the case of the mission-interrupting breakdowns every thirty-four miles, cited by Dina Rasor, the Army simply discounted many of the breakdowns from their calculations, announcing that the tank broke down "only" every 93.97 miles. On the battlefield, of course, breakdowns are breakdowns and not matters for adroit explanations.

Another way of upping test scores, it developed, was to assign tank crews much better qualified than the random personnel handling the tank in combat. Dina Rasor quoted an example of such score slanting in regard to bomber tests in a General Accounting Office report to the Congress: "In many cases, contractor personnel perform much of the required maintenance . . . above average Strategic Air Command pilots . . . were used during the B-1 [bomber] test program . . . Service maintenance personnel . . . were generally . . . much more highly qualified than personnel who will maintain the system after it is deployed."

When confronted with evidence of glaringly substandard test performances, the military has sometimes retreated behind the claim that "bugs" are normal in any weapons system—"that's what the tests are for." Once a bug surfaces, they say, it can be eliminated by a simple fix. In this way, major flaws that should have been picked up in the design and development phase persist into the production phase and even after, and have been explained away by the contractor as "normal."

The Stingless Viper: A Study in Megawaste

The Pentagon's trillion-dollar arms buildup is ostensibly aimed at bolstering the national security, but the combination of design and construction flaws, questionable decisions concerning actual needs, and sweetheart deals with contractors could have the effect of sapping America's vitality for generations to come. Against this background, the billion-dollar Viper rocket program seems insignificant; yet it calls for careful scrutiny, if only because it illustrates the assault on the nation's treasury and the incompetence connected to it.

With a flourish of trumpets, the Viper program was brought onstage in 1976. Its aim was to provide every American foot soldier with his own cheap, lightweight, shoulder-launched anti-tank rocket. The scenario was that infantrymen armed with Vipers would stalk the battlefields blowing away Soviet tanks and light fortifications. All this at an advertised cost of only $78 a weapon.

Admirable as was the intention, the Viper was compromised almost from the moment it left the drawing board. Warsaw Pact forces were being equipped with tanks whose heavy composite-steel frontal armor resisted Viper penetration. Meanwhile, the contractor, General Dynamics, managed within a few years to jump Viper's unit price from $78 to $787! The result was a costly and largely ineffective weapon against new-style tanks.

Faced with these basic facts, the Army redefined the standards by which the Viper was tested. It turned a deaf ear to critical report cards on Viper submitted by the General Accounting Office, the Office of Management and Budget, the Defense Resources Board, and an Army Select Committee. It professed complete mystification as to why the weapon's cost had risen so sharply. Above all, it angrily fought off criticism of Viper's contractor, General Dynamics, strongly affirming the company's status as the sole supplier of Vipers. Seemingly, the more Viper's shortcomings were laid bare, the more its use by American soldiers was assured.

Strangled in the Crib

Viper was a lineal descendant of the famous, deadly World War II rocket launcher called the bazooka (after the stovepipe-like musical instrument played by 1930s radio comedian Bob Burns). The weapon inspired a less-famous "son of bazooka," a light anti-tank rocket launcher called LAW. LAW proved a bust in Vietnam (it kept blowing up, and had a range of only 130 yards). But a captured Soviet version of the bazooka, the RPG-7, intrigued the American brass in Vietnam.

With due regard for the "grunt" infantryman who must lug at least forty-eight pounds of battle equipment into combat, the Army limited Viper's weight to a sparse seven pounds. It also specified that Viper should make no more noise than other battlefield weapons, which are limited to 180 decibels (higher noise levels ruin the hearing of combatants). Working within these noise and weight limitations, Army rocket experts had by 1974 come up with an ingenious Viper prototype—a forty-four-inch-long weapon firing a twenty-seven-inch-long rocket. It was about three inches in diameter, and accurate at up to 330 yards.

On hitting an enemy tank, the new rocket's warhead generated intense heat that theoretically could melt tank armor up to eighteen inches thick, enabling the exploding rocket to thrust through into the tank's interior. The casualties among the tank's crew were, of course, horrendous.

But now came a development reminiscent of what happened with the M-14 rifle, forerunner of the infamous M-16 rifle (see page 131). The Viper prototype was snatched away from the Army ordnance experts who had designed it, and was given over to the contractor, General Dynamics, for final development and manufacture.

General Dynamics ordnance people began by radically redesigning the fins that held the rocket steady in flight. The result was that the new fins scraped the inside of the "stovepipe" as the rocket missile whizzed through it. Having thus been slowed, the missile proved unstable when it emerged from the firing tube and encountered crosswinds. According to a revealing 1982 piece by Frank Greve, of the Knight-Ridder newspapers, it took General Dynamics six months to eliminate the flaw. A similar "fix" to cut down on the weapon's excessive noisiness cost $10 million.

As Viper's costs and fixes multiplied, the program became a revolving door for directors and deputy directors (five top managers in six years). Along the way, as mentioned earlier, the unit cost vaulted from $78 in 1975 to $787 in the early 1980s. The cost jumps were made so frequently that no one at General Dynamics could remember how the original $78 price tag had been arrived at. As a company executive put it rather primly, "Unfortunately, we don't have the institutional memory of 1975–76." This, in an age of unlimited computer memory. As in George Orwell's *1984*, unpleasant historical realities were simply willed out of existence.

With Viper's failures mounting and becoming common knowledge, General Dynamics personnel and their Army opposite numbers relied increasingly on imagination and ingenuity in coping with failure. Instead of testing how well Viper stood up to state-of-the-art tanks, the weapon was, according to Frank Greve, measured against relatively outmoded Soviet T-55 and T-62 tanks.

The next stacking-of-the-decks had to do with tests of Viper's ability to withstand immersion in water. The original minimum standard called for Viper to come up shooting accurately after being left for two hours in three feet of water, a requirement designed to surmount the problem of assault teams that might have to wade ashore in chest-deep water, or to crawl through swampy areas. Sad to say, the test revealed that the weapon malfunctioned after being under for two hours. But General Dynamics and Army brass came up with a Gordian-knot solution. They simply dropped the two-hour immersion requirement from the battery of tests.

On July 28, 1981, the General Accounting Office issued a report that said, in part, "Viper's demonstrated effectiveness barely meets the low end of the Army's requirements . . . Against the new tanks it will be facing, Viper remains largely ineffective." The report recommended firmly that Viper be scrapped. The Marine Corps concurred in this judgment. Nevertheless, the Army still gave strong backing to Viper, though several foreign firms had offered the U.S. similar anti-tank weapons costing, in one case, only a third as much as Viper.

Faced with overwhelming evidence that Viper warheads simply could not penetrate the frontal armor of the best Soviet tanks, the Army at last reacted. It recommended keeping Viper in production —with infantrymen using it to shoot at Soviet tanks *only from the side.* Critics were skeptical of this solution. It meant, they pointed out, that infantrymen would have to get within about 200 yards of Soviet tanks, then pop up and "Viperize" them. A clean miss or only a glancing hit would be tantamount to committing suicide, since when fired the Viper gives off a large puff of smoke clearly visible to enemy gunners. Even if the target were hit and knocked out, the Viper firer himself would become a target for other tanks, since they usually move about in groups, keeping a keen protective eye on each other. It therefore takes a cool hand indeed to launch a Viper.

Confronted by the appalling reality, Congress phased out the Viper in 1982. Meanwhile, of course, the American taxpayer had to foot the bill. But many critics of defense waste are alert to the possibility that the weapon may be buffed up, renamed, and reintroduced as the ultimate tank weapon.

The Pershing Missile: Up Like a Rocket . . .

West Germany's dazzling postwar economic performance is traceable, in large part, to America's generosity in supplying the wherewithal for Germany's defense umbrella. Because of this largesse, West Germany was able to divert vast sums to its civilian economy.

But what if key defense weapons supplied gratis by us were of dubious quality or were insufficiently tested? One such weapon is the much-vaunted Pershing 2, the giant American-donated, West German-based missile that is zeroed in on targets deep within the Soviet heartland. The German anti-nuclear movement's outrage is not entirely unfounded: If Pershing 2s should malfunction after launch, they might well rain down nuclear destruction on the host nation itself.

The accuracy of the Pershing 2 is not nearly such a demonstrated fact as the Pentagon would lead the German and American public to believe. On paper, the thirty-five-foot-long missile is entirely dependable: It is a veritable devil's workshop of nuclear explosive power capable of travelling 1,800 miles and, descending at 1,350 miles, landing within 120 feet of its target. Its "payload" is an explosion equal to that of twenty thousand tons of TNT. (The Pershing 2's predecessor, the Pershing 1A, had a range of only 400 miles and was accurate to only 1,500 feet, so it was of little use against the Soviet Union proper.)

It seems axiomatic that such a prodigiously destructive, radar-guided weapon should have been rigorously tested before being made a key ally's first line of defense against the world's second greatest power. Granted that 100 percent testing, complete with twenty megaton warheads, is not feasible, even partial testing would have been useful.

Yet Frank Greve quoted a congressional source as saying that Martin Marietta Corporation, which makes the missile, "is encountering very serious problems with its reliability and accuracy." In 1982, Defense Department Secretary Caspar Weinberger acknowledged before a congressional subcommittee that all was not well with the Pershing 2.

Critics contended that one reason for Pentagon reluctance to subject Pershing 2 to stringent testing was that in the late 1970s at White Sands, New Mexico, preliminary tests were unfavorable. In four out of five tries, Pershing 2 badly missed the target area. The testers then resorted to "rigging" tactics with the fifth attempt. A series of bright, head-high aluminum reflectors were installed along a line leading to the target. The signals bouncing back from the big reflectors were the equivalent of runway flares guiding a night-flying plane to a safe landing. Unfortunately, the enemy can't be expected to light the way to the target in future wars. More realistically, the enemy would probably create false mirror paths that would decoy missiles into landing elsewhere.

The experts' verdict on Pershing 2, therefore, was that it was vastly oversold to the Congress, and that it was hyped as meeting standards that were in fact "overambitious." In 1982, Secretary of the Army John R. Marsh wrote to a congressional subcommittee, "the government and the contractor were overly optimistic that [Pershing 2] would be a fairly simple Pershing variant. As the design of the system has matured, the manufacturing process has become more complex."

Despite its evident shortcomings, Pershing 2 has all along been pushed full-force by the Pentagon. In 1979, a not very eager Chancellor Helmut Schmidt said he would allow installation of Pershing 2s in West Germany. By 1987, a complement of 220 missiles should be in place in that country. And best of all, from the viewpoint of many in the military-industrial establishment, the weapon is providing a veritable gravy train: Budgeted at $1.8 billion in September 1981, Pershing 2's cost jumped $1 billion in just the next *three months*. This is believed to be the biggest short-term cost jump in the annals of Pentagon spending.

After the thirty-year pro-ICBM propaganda barrage laid down by the Pentagon, the American public must be forgiven if it honestly believes we can fly an intercontinental nuclear missile 6,000 miles, then drop it unerringly on target. The official claims are that we can send an ICBM from Southern California to the Marshall Islands in the South Pacific, then set it down in a lagoon within 600 feet of a target circle fifty-yards across. Since these ICBMs are advertised as the only thing deterring the Soviets from a first strike, the military doesn't believe we should cavil over the costs involved: It pushed long and hard for the controversial MX missile program, which carried a price tag of $34 billion.

Why should the Pentagon proclaim pinpoint intercontinental bombing accuracy that is non-existent? Those hyper-accurate missiles, they say, are designed "surgically" to snuff out enemy ICBM silos and other "limited" military targets. We have no interest, it is said, in vaporizing cities and large industrial concentrations, since we are opposed to "holocausts." In the slides-and-picture presentations the Pentagon puts on for notables, ICBMs are pictured as swift, sure, and safe. Boosted into near-space by multi-stage rockets, the missiles' warheads—rather demurely called "re-entry vehicles" in Pentagonese—are lifted to the outer fringes of the atmosphere, perhaps 150 miles up. At that point, the missile plunges back into the atmosphere at a speed of 12,000 miles an hour, moving along at a shallow angle. Going by purely internal instructions programmed into its computer "brain," the descending missile now lines up its warheads for their final dive to earth. Soon the last booster rocket burns out, and the warheads are on their own. From here on, they have no self-correcting features, such as signals from a mother ship. Silently, they drop toward the target as inert as a stone launched by a slingshot.

As the warhead streaks through the sea of air that forms the earth's atmosphere, its speed is slowed sharply, from 12,000 mph to about 1,350 mph on impact with earth. Along the way, the warhead encounters all sorts of disruptions. One disruption has to do with the earth's gravitational field. Since our planet is flattened at the poles and its internal makeup is highly varied—it is full of iron and stone deposits—the gravitational field also varies, unexpectedly. Knowing this, the navigational-guidance specialists who program missiles tried to anticipate gravitational anomalies, but it is impossible to compensate for all of them.

Other disruptions are caused by the churning, turbulent layers of air currents through which the missile is hurtling. The air over an icy countryside behaves differently from that over a warm forest land. Also, a solar flare can create dismaying atmospheric turbulence. So do thunderstorms and sudden shifts in barometric pressure.

The point is that all sorts of quirky forces pluck and tug at, or even buffet, a warhead as it descends. By the time it dives to earth, the warhead may be significantly off course. Scientists have calculated that a 180-knot jet stream 40,000 feet over the earth can deflect a warhead by as much as 1,065 feet. The "guidance" scientists can take approximate account of the jet stream when they are programming the missile's "brain," but the stream's speed itself fluctuates unpredictably. Against this background, it is not surprising that the most sophisticated "pre-packaging" cannot guarantee a warhead's arrival on dead center.

What about nuclear missiles launched from submarines much closer to enemy territory than land-based missiles? These missiles, are primarily designed to destroy cities rather than pin-pointed targets, for which they lack the calibrated accuracy.

Another theoretical possibility concerns stationary-orbit satellites—or the stars themselves—sending signals that make the missiles land squarely on targets. Such an approach sounds promising, but what if an enemy jams or otherwise interferes with these external signals? Could such electronic trickery even turn the ICBM around and send it back toward the nation from which it was launched?

Even "precision" bombing from planes—if they could get through Soviet defenses—might not do the trick against silos with relatively narrow "mouths" under their hardened-steel "manhole covers." In a 1980 *New York Review of Books* article, Alexander and Andrew Cockburn point out that even the Nagasaki bomb, dropped in broad daylight from an unopposed plane, did not land dead on target. At Bikini, in 1946, all systems were under control; yet the nuclear bomb missed the target by almost half a mile.

Commenting on the astonishing face-off between the nuclear superpowers, Dr. Richard Garwin of Cornell University has said, "If you cannot be sure that you would be able to hit the enemy's silos, then there is no point in even trying—because the idea is that one side could wipe out the other's missiles before they are launched in a first strike."

In the present state of things, the only military alternative to "surgical" first strikes at enemy silos is to "carpet bomb" an enemy with nuclear weapons. Such an operation means taking out all its cities and trusting that the sheer quantity of the bombs will ensure destruction of Soviet silos. But what if just a handful of high-megaton missiles survived these random blasts and rose from their silos to retaliate against America? We would have "won" the war, but would have lost the United States.

There remains, of course, a non-military alternative. We can try to arrange a mutual, rigidly inspected phasing-down of both countries' nuclear armamentarium. The technology for such an alternative exists. But this inevitably means that the vast sums now flowing to the military contractors will be sharply reduced or eliminated. And enough governmental power is now attached to the furnishing of those funds to make such a change a real test of public opinion. As both General Eisenhower and General MacArthur predicted, government cannot be depended upon to take the initiative in reversing the arms race. They contended that only an aroused public opinion could bring about such a vital change of direction.

The question, therefore, before Americans today is whether the main problem is understood by enough people and whether they can create the necessary mandate for government. Thomas Jefferson was right when he said that the glory of a free society is that its main direction must be charted by the people themselves.

10

General Dynamics

I n the early 1980s, General Dynamics had been riding high, its defense contracts accounting for 96.7 percent of its profits. With annual sales of almost $8 billion, the firm was America's third-biggest defense contractor (after McDonnell-Douglas and Rockwell International). The firm had 100,000 employees. Its fourteen busy divisions produced the awesome Trident nuclear submarines, F-16 Falcon fighter planes, battleships, space boosters, missiles, and supertankers. GD was so big and so "indispensable" that it was able to threaten to halt production of nuclear subs if the firm wasn't paid cost-overrun claims that eventually amounted to $844 million.

One day in 1983, a disgruntled General Dynamics vice-president, Takis Veliotis, left the company and began to talk openly of monumental dishonesty at GD, producing tapes and company documents. The eventual result was that GD was indicted, among other serious counts, for defrauding the government of many millions in cost-overrun charges. The Pentagon had no choice except to institute its own investigation. How could a firm as important as General Dynamics ever allow itself to perform practices that would expose it as a predator on the public treasury? The explanation has to do with the unreal world of the defense industry.

General Dynamics—an aristocrat among American defense contractors—could point to distinguished corporate bloodlines. One of

GD's "forebears" was New England's Quincy Shipbuilding Company, founded in 1893 by the noted electrical engineer T. A. Watson (to whom Alexander Graham Bell said, over the world's first telephone, "Mr. Watson, come here, I want you."). During World War II, Quincy's yards built 40 percent of our Navy's battleships, aircraft carriers, and destroyers. The slogan "Kilroy was here" traces to a wartime inspector named Kilroy, who used to scribble the phrase on the hulls of ships he had checked out.

Another GD ancestor was the Electric Boat Company, founded in 1899 by the American submarine pioneer John P. Holland. (The firm's Tom Swiftian name came from the fact that when submerged, the submarines it built ran on battery-powered engines.)

Both companies, along with dozens of others, were absorbed into the giant entity known as General Dynamics, founded in the 1950s. It hit its stride when Midwestern financier and board member Henry Crown persuaded David S. Lewis to become board chairman in 1970. Lewis had been head of McDonnell-Douglas, America's biggest defense contractor. Under Lewis, GD had fourteen divisions and was turning out Trident nuclear subs, F-16 Falcon fighter planes, M-1 Abrams tanks, Atlas space boosters, Tomahawk cruise missiles, and other state-of-the-art hardware. Like all modern arms makers, GD deliberately kept a low, almost invisible profile. So far as the public knew, it was just an honest, industrious manufacturer turning out complex war gear.

General Dynamics officials, however, were not unaware of the opportunities for maximizing profits in dealing with the U.S. government. Early on, the company began to overcharge for warships and planes—and then brazenly demanded reimbursement for "cost overruns."

Such treasury-raiding was not confined to any single program. Adm. Hyman G. Rickover, father of the nuclear submarine, asserted that GD had made fraudulent claims on its submarine-building programs. William Howard Taft IV, deputy defense secretary, deplored GD's "bad claims," and called the corporation "the worst offender." A shocked official of the U.S. Maritime Agency, which had contributed $81 million to GD's building of some tankers, said,

"The profits to General Dynamics were the highest ever on a ship subsidized by the maritime administration." As stated earlier, Pentagon auditor and whistle-blower Ernest Fitzgerald estimated that overcharges by defense firms such as GD amounted to at least $30 billion a year. Not surprisingly, General Dynamics sailed along for years, collecting overrun megapayments without paying a cent in federal income taxes.

In the early 1970s, the company was bent on obtaining a contract to build SSN-688 attack submarines. Testimony, however, revealed that GD knew it could not deliver the subs at a time and at a price acceptable to the government. According to later charges, GD simply quoted a too-low price and a too-fast delivery date. Further, it told the Pentagon that GD would make only a modest 10 percent profit on the contract, although the firm's private projections clearly indicated a profit at least three times higher. All this, of course, was illegal, especially since the "real" projections were calmly entered in a separate set of secret books. But the ruse worked: General Dynamics got the contract, later making up for the artificially low price by billing the government for its monstrous cost overruns (which it blamed on the *Navy*'s inefficiency). As for the imminently looming delivery date, GD simply put the Navy off with ingenious excuses, and finally delivered the subs *two years* after the deadline. Total cost to the taxpayers: $2.5 billion.

This whole routine calls to mind a joke that accountants tell on themselves. A businessman boasts, "You know how I located a good accountant? I called six of the top accountants and asked them, 'What does two plus two equal?' They all said four, so I hung up on them. Finally I called a seventh accountant and asked him. He said, 'What do you *want* two and two to equal?' I knew then that I had my man!" Possibly GD heard this joke and hired the seventh accountant. Senator William Proxmire said of these and other alleged GD transactions, "documented facts indicate a systematic pattern of deceitful conduct . . . It's far more serious than even I imagined."

But where, in all this, was our vaunted safety net—the army of watchdog agencies that in theory keep a beady eye on government disbursements? Congress, the Pentagon, and the Executive maintain a dense network of supposedly ever-vigilant auditors and investigators to sniff out fiscal malfeasance. We have, among others, the Defense Contract Audit Agency, the Defense Procurement Fraud Unit, the House and Senate armed forces committees' watchdog units, the Securities and Exchange Commission, the General Accounting Office, and the Defense Criminal Investigating Service.

The Navy, for instance, assigns inspecting officers to Plant Representative Offices—NAVPROS, in Navalese—which are located right on the working floor of a defense contractor's factory. These officers make the rounds, constantly checking out the quality of the product and the performance of the civilian personnel. NAVPROS are the Pentagon-based contract officer's eyes and ears on the scene. As one insider put it, "NAVPROS are where the rubber meets the road." In addition, the Pentagon deploys platoons of auditors who double-check all production reports, alert to the slightest discrepancy between a contractor's projections and the actual production figures. Surely, no wrongdoer can penetrate this array of mine fields?

But General Dynamics—like other big-time contractors—knew how to pick its way through the mine fields. The techniques that worked best came under three main headings: The Revolving Door strategy, the "perks and good fellowship" gambit, and the Blackmail ploy.

By far the most effective of these techniques was the Revolving Door strategy, which is to say, personnel involved in awarding contracts who later turn up in high-salaried executive positions in the firms they favored. The most celebrated Revolving Door cases were those of Edward Hidalgo and George Sawyer. In 1976, General Dynamics put in overrun claims on the SSN-688 attack subs; in the end, the claims came to $844 million. Despite awareness in Pentagon circles that the claims were fraudulent, Hidalgo—who was then Navy secretary—settled the matter by arranging for a $642 million payment. Sawyer, a Pentagon official, soothed GD even further by awarding it $5 billion in new contracts. Hidalgo later joined General Dynamics as a handsomely paid legal consultant, and Sawyer became a GD vice-president. Both men maintained that their megabuck decisions in favor of GD had in no way been influenced by expectations of their later jobs. But cynics make the point that in one three-year period 3,200 Pentagon officers with the rank of major or higher left their jobs in order to jump to defense firms—GD very much among them. Even this figure is, it turns out, sharply understated.

Many of the "jumpers" to defense firms were once PROS— high-ranking armed services personnel assigned to Plant Representative Offices. In a remarkable series of articles keyed to the General Dynamics scandal in the *St. Louis Post-Dispatch,* Bob Adams wrote that these "plant reps" usually "go over and kick the tires, test the ignition, twist the steering wheel, rub their fingers on the paint . . . If everything is okay, they write a check." If someone on a tire-kicking squad got too frisky and began writing reports that were too picky, he was made to know that his chances of landing a soft post-retirement job with the host firm (or any other defense firm) were negligible.

Even if plant reps had no Revolving Door aspiration, there was always the palship syndrome. As Adams puts it, plant reps and plant employees "drive to work in the same car pools, jog at the same company health club . . . [and may] have relatives working for the contractor." *Post-Dispatch* writer Karen L. Koman adds of the reps at McDonnell-Douglas, "They eat in the same cafeteria, they play slow pitch softball against McDonnell teams. The Navy people are free to join any of the numerous McDonnell 'clubs,' such as the ski club or the video club."

In this environment of dawn-to-midnight conviviality, it was easy for a plant rep to develop unprofessional, pro-contractor sympathies.

The Revolving Door syndrome was not confined to on-line reps and Pentagon biggies. It was commonplace, for instance, for lawyers with the Justice Department Defense Procurement Fraud Unit to yield to attractive employment offers from firms they were investigating or prosecuting. The first director of the fraud unit, Richard A. Sauber, moved to a Washington law firm famous for defending big-time defense contractors under government investigation. Another case: Thomas Edwards, once head of the U.S. Attorney's fraud division in New York, ended up in 1981 defending General Dynamics against fraud investigations.

General Dynamics officials used the "sole source" argument to strengthen their position. Yet everyone in Defense knew that "sole source" General Dynamics subcontracted its work out to dozens of small businesses. American industry is, in fact, in large part based on the concept that interchangeable parts can be manufactured anywhere, once the exact specifications of the product are supplied. These same Pentagon officials who allowed GD's supposed "sole source" capability to serve as a rationale for by-passing genuine competitive bidding were driving cars whose high-tech components were made in different locales, then brought together for final assembly. A little-publicized case is relevant here. During an investigation it came out that GD had charged the government $14,835 for two specialized alignment pins used on aircraft that were actually worth only $45 a pair. GD also billed the government $9,609 for a socket wrench. Given the specs, the Air Force facilities duplicated the wrench for $105. So much for the "sole source" myth: It is, as the French say, a lie agreed upon. No wonder Pentagon whistle-blower Ernest Fitzgerald mused, "When you see a beautiful plane flying overhead, you are literally watching a set of overpriced spare parts flying together in close formation."

Though the threat to stop production is highly effective, there is an even deadlier form of pressure. At least forty-eight of the states have defense plants that provide a good living for many thousands of people. A reflection of this fact was evident in the 1983 military budget request for a record-breaking $239 billion. Even the Senate was taken aback by this huge figure, and grumbling was heard. As the grumbling swelled in volume, Senator John Tower of Texas, ever the great good friend of the Pentagon, sat by looking bemused. Finally he lowered the boom. As writer Margaret Freivogel told the story in the *St. Louis Post-Dispatch* series on Pentagon waste, Tower, "then chairman of the Senate Armed Services Committee, invited his colleagues to suggest cuts—from their own states. The silence was deafening. Only a handful of the senators dared to suggest reductions that would hurt their own constituents."

The nightmare prospect of large-scale reductions in funds for the states brought on by close-downs of defense plants is the one biggest ally of the defense contractors. Whenever congressional lions get to roaring about Pentagon extravagance, the slightest mention of local benefits is enough to silence the budget cutters. *St. Louis Post-Dispatch* reporter Freivogel comments: "Companies [build] supports for projects by lining up subcontractors . . . in 48 states. The M-1 Abrams tank has them in 40 states."

What this means is that America is allowing itself to become a nation dependent on defense megadollars. Defense plants must be kept going lest the folks back home suffer agonizing withdrawal pangs. Like streetcorner drug pushers, the Pentagon-Congress-Contractor troika makes America acquiescent by threatening to hold back on the country's "supply."

Fortunately, America has a way of producing unlikely heroes and heroines who, in crises, dare to speak truth to power. For years before GD was finally indicted in 1985, a brave irregular army of watchdogs were protesting the firm's overpricing and misrepresentations. In addition to the whistle-blowers mentioned in an earlier chapter, there are Senator William Proxmire, Representative J. D. Dingell, and the many anonymous "Pentagon underground" personnel who risked their careers by exposing GD's goings-on.

For some time, even these brave efforts had only mixed effects. The reason, for the most part, was that the Pentagon and various congressional committees either cold-shouldered or actually stiff-armed the whistle-blowers, or subjected their claims to slow-motion, foot-dragging inquiries that predictably came to nothing. If "stiff-armed" seems too strong a description, consider this: The Pentagon more than once flatly refused Senator Grassley permission to speak to one of its employees about defense overspending. Anyone who knows how the Pentagon goes out of its way to accommodate members of Congress knows how unusual are the rebuffs to Grassley. As stated earlier, Senator Grassley routinely asked the Justice Department for documents relating to Justice's half-hearted "investigation" of Admiral Rickover's charges against General Dynamics. Displaying a decisiveness and crisp authority conspicuously absent from its investigation of GD, the department flatly refused. When the undaunted Grassley threatened to institute contempt-of-Congress proceedings, the documents were grudgingly forthcoming. It was through such dogged research that Grassley unearthed data on the now-famous $7,622 coffee brewer and the $745 pair of pliers.

By the early 1980s, General Dynamics was still riding high, having successfully fended off numerous charges of fraud and overpricing in its dealings with the government. But the air was still heavy with allegations only awaiting the lightning stroke that would bring them raining down. The lightning came when in 1983 Takis Veliotis resigned his post as GD vice-president and fled the United States. Settling in Greece, Veliotis began blowing the whistle on his old company; down came the deluge.

The background to this astonishing episode was that Veliotis—the head of GD's submarine-building Electric Boat division in Connecticut—had been indicted on charges that he had shaken down a GD subcontractor for $1.35 million. (Ironically, GD, the great exponent of "sole source" contracts, had farmed out $44 million worth of work to this subcontractor!) Determined not to be made a scapegoat in the shakedown case, the self-exiled Veliotis now blew the whistle to Justice Department investigators, in hopes of getting lenient treatment for turning state's evidence. What made Veliotis's charges credible was that he backed them up with company documents and tape recordings of conversations with officials. On a recording made in the 1970s, a top GD executive confided to Veliotis that GD chairman David S. Lewis lied to the government about the delivery date of some Trident nuclear subs. Lewis's reason: "to keep [GD] stock price from sliding." Another document showed that GD had given more than $67,000 in jewelry and other gifts to, of all people, the father of the nuclear submarine, Adm. Hyman G. Rickover. Under GD's bookkeeping system, the gifts were charged off to another account. Veliotis's revelations had an electrifying effect on official Washington—especially on agencies that had in the past been openly lackadaisical about investigating GD, including the Securities and Exchange Commission. Meanwhile, congressional watchdogs who had long been obstructed and snickered at for challenging

GD's actions got their second wind. Representative John Dingell's doughty House Energy and Commerce Committee opened new hearings on GD. (With help from his ace senior investigator, Peter Stockton, Dingell was at last able to obtain the document that showed the firm had cynically charged Uncle Sam $320,000 for Chairman Lewis's plane trips to his country home in Georgia.) Senator William Proxmire's Joint Economic Committee began holding hearings on GD's submarine contracts. Senator Charles Grassley brought his Judiciary Subcommittee into the fray. Even the Defense Department was moved to say it was keeping a stern eye on the situation.

A Legend is Toppled

To make an airtight legal case, various committees focussed on two relatively minor areas (no doubt remembering that Al Capone was prosecuted not for murder but for tax evasion). These areas were GD's documented gifts to Rickover, and the firm's alleged highly illegal juggling of its books in connection with the submarine contracts.

The anti-corruption forces won the Rickover action, but it was a bittersweet victory. Brilliant and abrasive, the eighty-five-year-old admiral had long been a tireless foe of billion-dollar corruption in defense contracting, and he had the enemies to prove it. The Washington rumor mills had been grinding out reports that the defense establishment tried to force Rickover to retire from the Navy in 1982 not because of his advanced age but because of their rage at his threat to their "take." Still, improbably, the Veliotis documents did show that between 1961 and 1977, Rickover had accepted from GD gifts to the value of $67,628. The gifts turned out to be an odd mixture of jade earrings, fruit knives, ditty bags, teak trays, and similar kitschy items. Rickover protested that all these items except the jewelry were mere commemorative trinkets that he had passed on to defense-establishment colleagues as souvenirs. He had given the jewels to his wife. The Navy Gratuities Board that sat on the case recommended the softest possible punishment.

In a fine display of outrage, Navy Secretary John F. Lehman in May 1985 cracked down on GD with a $676,280 fine—the standard punishment of ten times the amount of any bribe given. Lehman also suspended new contracts for two GD divisions. And he sent Rickover a blistering letter of censure, rebuking him for taking bribes. However, Senator Proxmire, the Hill's traditional foe of corruption, defended Rickover and called Lehman's action excessive.

Both Proxmire and Dingell criticized the Navy's reaction to the scandal itself as curiously weak. The "suspension" of GD was quietly lifted a few months later, in August 1985.

The Sledgehammer Descends

The fallout from the Veliotis revelations kept raining down: David S. Lewis, still stonewalling all the way, was forced out as GD chairman. In December 1985, a federal grand jury indicted General Dynamics and three of its executives. The charges concerned an alleged GD conspiracy to defraud the government in work done on the ill-fated DIVAD anti-aircraft gun (later called the Sergeant York gun—see p. 123). The identity of a fourth indictee was a shocker: James M. Beggs, a General Dynamics executive during the Sergeant York days, who had gone on to become chief administrator of NASA and the top figure in America's space program. The indictments charged that GD "ran over" on the Sergeant York costs, then covered the loss by overcharging the government on other accounts. The indictment—one count of conspiracy and six counts concerning false statements—was serious business. Each count, if sustained, might mean a $10,000 fine and five years in jail for each defendant. For this reason, the General Dynamics trial—originally scheduled for April 1986, but repeatedly postponed until October 1986—attracted deep interest among both friends and foes of waste. According to government lawyer Randy I. Bellows, the prosecution was gathering for this trial about three million pages of evidence, and it intended to call at least seventy witnesses.

Meanwhile, General Dynamics seemed to be riding out the storm rather tidily. Late in 1985, the Department of Defense had barred the firm from any dealings with the Navy, pending outcome of the trial. But in February 1986, the ever-forgiving Navy had jumped the gun by ending the debarment. This was possible, the Pentagon explained, because GD had thoroughly reformed itself, and had set up a system of rigorous checks to prevent future wrongdoing. The reforms included new auditing and monitoring procedures and mandatory attendance by employees at "ethics seminars." GD's new chairman, Frank Pace, former secretary of the Army, said that the firm's reinstatement in no way implied a return to the old carefree days. GD had in effect been placed, he said, on strict probation. The surveillance and monitoring agreed to by GD was unprecedented in the defense community.

As if to underscore GD's new probationary status, Navy Assistant Secretary Everett Pyatt disclosed in February 1986 that the Pentagon was still carrying on between ten and fifteen separate investigations of General Dynamics.

The Malignancy Within

What are we to make of the General Dynamics affair? To paraphrase an editorial in *The New York Times,* in the name of fighting socialism we have ourselves become a socialistic "junkie" state, morbidly dependent for our economic well-being on cozy arrangements rationed out to the big contractors by the Pentagon and Congress. Senator David Pryor of Arkansas made this point forthrightly when he said, "The Pentagon today is the biggest socialistic empire in the United States." It is an empire that sucks up two-thirds of the country's annual revenues and paralyzes our will to resist internal inefficiency, waste, and incompetence.

It would be a mistake to assume that the General Dynamics

scandals apply only to GD or are solely the product of a few misguided or predatory corporation officials who perceive easy opportunities to aggrandize their company. The General Dynamics frauds are inherent in an underlying situation in which defense policy and foreign policy become so intertwined that the nation has a stake in world tensions. When massive military spending becomes institutionalized, a wide range of factors comes into play to keep it going. Ultimately, the danger is not that military spending no longer is the adjunct of foreign policy, but that foreign policy becomes the adjunct of military spending. It is here that the pathology of power becomes not only most manifest but most dangerous.

A Guide to Star Wars

ASAT

Anti-Satellite. Any weapon or system capable of destroying a satellite, usually military or communications satellites.

DETERRENCE

A strategy to prevent hostile nuclear attacks by threat of retaliation or by defense against incoming missiles.

FIRST STRIKE

The capability of one side to attack the other with such devastating force that the nation suffering the attack would lose its ability to retaliate.

LASER

Light Amplification by the Stimulation of Electromagnetic Radiation.

MIRV

Multiple Independently Targeted Reentry Vehicle. Each vehicle has more than one warhead independently programmed by its own computers to hit separate targets.

MISSILE

A self-propelling, unmanned weapon.

ABM

Anti-Ballistic Missile, which intercepts any missile whether sea- or land-launched.

CRUISE

Small, unmanned airplanes carrying either nuclear or non-nuclear warheads. They can be launched from air, ground, or sea, and can be guided all the way to their targets.

ICBM

Intercontinental Ballistic Missile. ICBMs are land-based, long-range weapons, some having a range of 6,000 miles.

MX

Missile Experimental, or "Peacekeeper." The MX carries ten warheads.

SLBM

Submarine-Launched Ballistic Missile.

SS-18

Soviet ICBM which contains ten nuclear warheads.

SALT I

Strategic Arms Limitation Treaty of 1972, which produced the ABM Treaty restricting ABM systems, and a five-year interim agreement limiting missile launchers.

SALT II

Strategic Arms Limitation Treaty of 1979, which put a ceiling on intercontinental-range bombers and missile launchers, including multiple warhead launchers. It was not ratified by the U.S. Senate, but both the U.S. and the USSR agreed to abide by its provisions.

SDI

Strategic Defense Initiative, or "Star Wars."

SIOP

Single Integrated Operating Plan. A contingency plan for fighting and enduring a limited nuclear war.

11

Star Wars

I n the words of George F. Kennan, former ambassador to the Soviet Union and formulator of U.S. containment policy, ". . . there is no issue at stake in our political relations with the Soviet Union—no hope, no fear, nothing to which we aspire, nothing we would like to avoid—which could conceivably be worth a nuclear war. And . . . there is no way in which nuclear weapons could conceivably be employed in combat that would not involve the possibility—and indeed the prohibitively high probability—of escalation into a general nuclear disaster." The reasoning behind this statement is clear. The Second World War produced perhaps the greatest single change in the history of nations. With the development of atomic explosives, war became obsolete as an instrument of national policy.

In one way or another, almost all the world's leaders accepted the new reality. Winston Churchill declared that a world government represented the best chance for protecting the human race against an unspeakable catastrophe. Dwight D. Eisenhower asserted that the only alternative to world war was world law. John F. Kennedy called for a peace race to end the arms race. Pope John XXIII believed that a nuclear war would not be a war of nation against nation but a war of man against God, for such a war would smash at the conditions of life itself. Jawaharlal Nehru said that human beings could not claim they were truly civilized unless they outgrew the habit of war. Nine words epitomized the new condition in the world: *The only defense in an atomic age is peace.*

If this basic truth is to serve as the imperative for foreign policy, it would mean that the underlying principle of U.S. foreign policy would be centered on the need to create a workable world order. In it, the nations would retain sovereignty in all those matters relating to internal problems and institutions while accepting the jurisdiction of a responsible world body in disputes beyond their borders. This division of sovereignty or authority is what is meant by the principle of federalist organization, best described by the architects of the United States Constitution.

The attempt to find a workable way to abolish war, however, is only half of what is implied in the contention that the only defense against nuclear war is peace. The development of the world's resources for the world's good, together with a campaign against hunger and squalor, are the indispensable requirements of a planet safe and fit for human habitation.

The basic fallacy of the Strategic Defense Initiative, or "Star Wars," is that it runs directly counter to the central meaning and mandate of the atomic age. It throws us back to pre-atomic thinking. It assumes that nuclear war is survivable—even though President Reagan has declared that a "nuclear war cannot be won and must never be fought."

The arguments behind "Star Wars" are prime symptoms of the pathology of power. The central argument is that it is theoretically possible, from stations in space, to intercept and destroy attacking missiles before they reach their American targets. It becomes important, therefore, to examine this hypothesis. Even assuming the operational success of a device in space that can attack incoming missiles, some military experts have pointed out that an enemy could penetrate the system by flooding the skies with decoys or unarmed missiles as a prelude to attack. No "Star Wars" advocate has contended that all missiles could be intercepted. If only a small fraction of the invading missiles were to penetrate the defenses, a large number of American cities could be devastated.

Next, it is argued that "Star Wars" is exclusively defensive in nature. Military scientists have been quick to point out that the lasers on these space vehicles could produce vast firestorms in the cities below, making lasers as efficient at destroying population centers as the missiles they were intended to intercept.

Implied in the "Star Wars" argument is the assumption that the United States can gain a significant military advantage over the Soviet Union. This same argument was used to justify every new weapon development since the end of the Second World War. After the atomic bomb was dropped on Hiroshima, many of the scientists who helped develop that explosive tried to educate the American people to the reality that the U.S. atomic monopoly could not last. They urged the government to take advantage of our temporary atomic superiority by pressing for effective controls in an effort to head off an atomic armaments race. But the contrary assumption—that even if the U.S. monopoly were broken, the United States would be so far ahead that the Soviet Union could never catch up—persisted and prevailed. The result of this policy was that, when the Soviet Union developed its own atomic explosives, the fact of larger and more sophisticated U.S. stockpiles provided no comfort for Americans in view of the obvious fact that only a limited number of such explosives could accomplish an enemy's objectives.

At every step along the way, efforts to halt or turn back the arms race were defeated, not just by Soviet intransigence, but by those forces within the United States that never accepted the proposition that American security was tied to the control of force rather than the pursuit of force. The same fallacious thinking is apparent in the pressure to proceed with "Star Wars" regardless of the volatile element it will add to the arms race.

Much of the debate over "Star Wars" has been directed to its scientific feasibility—whether it is in fact possible to devise a space-based system of detecting and knocking down attacking missiles within seconds of their launching. The main issue in the debate, however, should not be whether the technological problems can be solved, but what happens if indeed the problems *are* solved. Is it any less certain that the USSR will be able to develop its own counterpart or counteractive weapons? If it does, will the net result be greater or less security for the United States?

Shortly after President Ronald Reagan returned from his meeting with Premier Mikhail Gorbachev of the Soviet Union in Geneva in 1985, he reported on his trip to a Maryland high school audience. "I couldn't help but say to him [Gorbachev]," the president told his listeners, "just think how easy his task and mine might be if suddenly there was a threat to this world from some other species from another planet outside in the universe. We'd forget all the little local differences that we have between our countries and we would find out once and for all that we really are all human beings here on this Earth together."

The youngsters who heard this statement might well have wondered why the leaders of their societies should have to wait for an extra-terrestrial invasion before recognizing the need to resolve differences and to arrive at a level of common safety. Nor could the schoolchildren be blamed if they concluded that psychological factors, rather than ideology or other supposedly intrinsic problems, are at the heart of the volatile antagonisms in the world today.

The president also spoke to his high school audience about "Star Wars." He said it provided both countries with a potential breakthrough in defensive weaponry that could put an end to the terror of nuclear war. He said he told Premier Gorbachev that "men of good will should be rejoicing that our deliverance from the awful threat of nuclear weapons may be on the horizon."

Scientists began calling attention to the fact that these new "weapons of peace" have *offensive* capabilities hardly less devastating than those represented by nuclear explosives. As pointed out a moment ago, the same mammoth lasers that are designed to intercept and destroy intercontinental ballistic missiles (ICBMs) could disintegrate cities within minutes, producing raging fires over hundreds of miles. A January 1986 article in *Physics and Society* warned that the levels of smoke generated by massive fires ignited by the new space weapons could be comparable to the amounts of dust and smoke resulting from a major nuclear exchange, therefore potentially causing a "nuclear winter," subfreezing global temperatures that would kill ecosystems and, possibly, all human life.

During World War II, the fires caused by the bombing of Germany and Japan were mainly responsible for the high civilian death toll. Similarly, at Hiroshima and Nagasaki, most of the casualties were the result of uncontrollable fires caused by the atomic bomb, rather than the blast. One reason why air raid shelters do not offer adequate protection in a nuclear war is that the firestorms consume the surface oxygen. Air drawn from the outside converts the shelters into incinerators. In the arguments for "Star Wars," no mention is made of its destructive power against population centers.

According to a classified study by R and D Associates, an influential defense think tank based in California, limited *laser* strikes could eliminate conventional forces such as bombers, tanks, and military installations while keeping collateral damage to a minimum —an idea which would appeal to those in favor of limited *nuclear* strikes. However, should the Soviets acquire a defensive system of their own, the U.S. would be subject to the same kind of attack.

"Anything that involves large amounts of energy can be used for good or evil purposes," said Dr. John D. G. Rather, vice-president of the Kaman Aerospace Corporation, in a *New York Times* article of March 7, 1985. "A system of space battle stations designed to stop a nuclear attack also may have the potential to attack selected targets in space, in the atmosphere or down on the surface of the earth." The "Star Wars" defense "shield" may, in fact, become a new space "weapon" and represent a hazardous escalation of the arms race.

The president's enthusiasm for "Star Wars" is at variance with two government-sponsored studies, one by his own Commission on Strategic Forces, headed by Retired Air Force Lt. Gen. Brent Scowcroft, and another for the Office of Technology Assessment, by Ashton B. Carter of the Massachusetts Institute of Technology. These studies agreed that a "total" defense against ballistic missile attack is neither technically feasible nor cost-effective. In addition, a Pentagon study headed by Fred S. Hoffman of Pan Heuristics, a California-based think tank, described the administration's goals as sufficiently unlikely to be achieved to warrant focussing on more moderate objectives.

Despite this background, "Star Wars" was to become the fastest growing and costliest single research undertaking in American history. It gained a lot of support from the argument that the Soviet Union had three times more land-based ICBMs than the U.S. What this argument ignored was the fact that the United States had an even more important advantage in sea-launched ballistic missiles and long-range bombers. The advantage was three to one. The U.S. deliberately opted for this approach rather than emphasizing land-based ICBMs because it guaranteed the ability to retaliate in the event of a surprise attack. Fixed targets are always theoretically vulnerable.

Most international military experts consider the U.S. to be equal if not superior in military capability to the Soviet Union. American military experts, if pressed, would not want to eliminate the asymmetries in the arsenals of both countries. Paul Warnke, former head of the Arms Control and Disarmament Agency and chief SALT II negotiator, observed that ". . . you can find a lot of critics of SALT pointing to the fact that 75 percent of their force is bigger than 30 percent of ours. But if we compare 100 percent against 100 percent, we have the better forces and we have the more survivable forces. And SALT preserves that. They talk about the fact that the Soviets were allowed to keep their 308 heavy missiles. We don't have heavy missiles because we don't want them. We could have made the MX as big as the SS-18 [a Soviet missile]."

Assertions of U.S. inferiority, according to Gerard Smith, chief SALT I negotiator under President Nixon, "raise questions about the [Reagan] Administration's common sense, and worse, its credibility . . . Until now, negotiations had been based on the assumption that a situation of parity existed between the two parties. It will take some doing to arrive at [arms control] arrangements that correct a balance now alleged to be out of equilibrium."

The drumbeats about the Soviet threat began in 1976 when a group of outside consultants called "Team B" were invited by the head of the CIA to review classified documents in order to reassess

Soviet military strength. Although earlier CIA findings concluded that a state of relative military parity existed between the United States and the Soviet Union, Team B found the Soviets to be militarily superior and intent on retaining their advantage. Its reassessment was used to justify a rapid arms build-up.

Team B eventually evolved into the Committee on the Present Danger (CPD), many key members of which later occupied influential positions in the Reagan administration. Convinced that the Soviets are bent on world domination, the CPD argued that arms control treaties locked the U.S. into weakness. They are opposed to any negotiations that would result in reduced military spending. They justify their fears by pointing to references in Soviet military literature to plans for fighting and surviving a nuclear war, ignoring the fact that our military manuals point in the same direction and speak in the same matter-of-fact tones. Since 1960, our manuals have included SIOP (Single Integrated Operating Plan), a contingency plan for fighting and enduring a limited nuclear war. What is expected of American military planners must also be expected of Soviet military planners.

"Star Wars" has profited from what some scientists feel have been selective and exaggerated leaks of highly classified information suggesting the success of new weapons technology. For example, in September 1985, the governmental Strategic Defense Initiative Organization hailed the chemical laser's destruction of an old Titan I missile shell. According to *Los Angeles Times* writer Robert Scheer, "A high-powered rifle would have done the same." Another highly publicized success was the explosion of a mock Soviet SS-18 missile caused by pellets shot from a "rail gun" which turned out to be a contemporary version of an eighteenth-century "light gas" gun. Concerned scientists such as physicist William L. Morgan, of the Lawrence Livermore National Laboratory, have been expressing their frustration with classification rules which prevent them from supplying accurate data that reflect the genuine status of "Star Wars" research. Morgan countered bold hyperbolizations made by his colleagues Edward Teller and Lowell Wood: "To lie to the public because we know that the public doesn't understand all this technical stuff brings us scientists down to the level of hawkers of snake oil, miracle cleaners, and Veg-o-Matics."

As pointed out earlier, no major weapons system ever developed has been withheld from deployment. Robert Scheer summed up the problem in *With Enough Shovels: Reagan, Bush and Nuclear War*: "The weapons technology keeps evolving, scientific breakthroughs occur, and just when it no longer seems possible, yet another new weapon or a new defensive system is born. It must then be developed —lest the enemy acquire the technology and, with it, a commanding lead in the arms race." Politicians and scientists have both capitalized on this phenomenon.

Research on "Star Wars" by government scientists has been pursued by applying a layered approach to the "Star Wars" system. The first layer of defense is directed against missiles during their boost phase—a three- to five-minute flight in the earth's atmosphere. The second layer of the defense attacks both the post-boost vehicle (which contains the warheads) as well as the warheads themselves after they have been dispensed. This phase can last up to twenty-five minutes for an ICBM or as little as three to five minutes for a Sea-Launched Ballistic Missile (SLBM). The final layer of the defense attacks the warheads during the last minute or two of their flight as they reenter the earth's atmosphere (filtering out the lighter decoys in the process).

Boost phase interception is prerequisite to an effective defense from ballistic missiles for several reasons: First, missile destruction in this phase is most efficient. Once a Soviet missile has passed the boost phase it becomes a pack of up to ten warheads, or reentry vehicles, and up to 100 or more decoys (e.g., lightweight aluminized plastic-covered balloons having the same appearance and motion as warheads in the absence of friction above the earth's atmosphere). Second, the intensity of infrared radiation emitted from boost-phase missile exhaust permits easy detection and targeting at a large distance. Third, because the booster rocket is larger and more fragile than the warheads they release, missile destruction is easiest during the boost phase. Fourth, no viable concept has yet been devised for a highly effective middle-layer defense against thousands of warheads and decoys, and, unfortunately, last-minute interception of incoming warheads at high altitudes can still devastate our cities.

The immutable laws of nature mandate that boost-phase interception take place from the vantage point of space because the earth is round and launched ICBMs cannot be targeted from the horizon. This is why "Star Wars" is to be largely space-based. Since early interception is so critical, laser weapons are being most heavily considered because they operate at the speed of light.

There are two different methods for accomplishing a space-based defensive attack. One is to place weapons on orbiting battle stations just above the edge of the earth's atmosphere. The other is to have the system launched into space on cue from early warning satellites. Because of the speed of today's offensive weaponry, should either space-based mode be made to work, it would of necessity eliminate human decision-making time.

Each proposed system possesses its own unique set of disadvantages. However, the main problem with weapons systems being based in space is their vulnerability to direct attack or paralysis from high altitude explosions, particularly if an enemy mounts his own ballistic missile defense. Furthermore, equipment in low orbit (at the edge of earth's atmosphere, approximately sixty-two miles above ground) would continuously be circling and would thus require massive duplication (by the 100s) to ensure adequate coverage of enemy missile silos. Even so, for all the circulating weapons platforms, only a few at any given time may be available to defend against an onslaught of ballistic missiles. And, unfortunately, a good offense could put those few weapons platforms out of commission, allowing penetration of the first layer of defense. Additionally, the cost of placing so many devices into orbit would be enormous due to the expense of large energy requirements, transportation of fuel and equipment into space, operations, and servicing—not including research, development, and construction costs.

Although defensive weapons "popped up" from the ground possess the advantage of reduced vulnerability and greater efficiency, they are severely hampered by time constraints. A study of defensive technologies, directed by James C. Fletcher, administrator of

NASA, has reported that it is possible to build ICBMs that complete their boost phase in as little as forty seconds without making many compromises in the destructive value of the bombs. It has been estimated that interception by a laser-type "pop-up" system would take about 120 seconds at best. Further holding up interception time would be battle management systems which require time to perform and submarines (most likely to launch these "pop-up" systems because of their proximity to the enemy targets), which cannot launch all missiles at once. This predicament is perilous for submarines in that they are vulnerable to detection after first firing.

The only candidate light enough to play a "pop-up" defensive role is the nuclear-powered X-ray laser, considered to be one of the most promising of the new "Star Wars" technologies. The energy from a nuclear explosion is channeled into laser beams destroying objects at large distances by hitting them with a strong shock wave. X-ray beams are very wide and encompass an area much larger than the target; thus they destroy more quickly and require less accuracy and tracking time than other laser weapons do. However, the X-ray laser possesses several disadvantages. It cannot penetrate the earth's atmosphere; therefore it is effective only in space. It is also nuclear driven—requiring up to twelve times the tonnage of the Hiroshima bomb—and may be as hazardous as the missiles it seeks to intercept. This poses an uncomfortable dilemma for an administration that bills "Star Wars" as "non-nuclear." In addition, the X-ray laser is able to fire only once before consuming itself—calling into question whether or not it should only be launched against an appropriately large barrage.

A hybrid system that includes both ground- and space-based components has been proposed in an effort to escape the drawbacks of space-based and "pop-up" systems. A ground-based excimer laser beam of intense ultraviolet light would be directed toward a large mirror high in geosynchronous orbit—an orbit in which objects travel in sync with the earth approximately 22,000 miles above the equator. The laser beam would reflect onto smaller "fighting" mirrors in low orbit that would in turn aim the beam toward its target. The short wavelength light emitted by an excimer laser beam makes it a good candidate for focusing at a very long range. This two-mirror scheme would reduce the beam diffraction caused by distance and could produce enough focus to destroy a missile. Because such a system requires no heavy equipment and energy sources in space —only mirrors—it is less vulnerable to attack and more efficient than solely space-based systems. The transmission of laser beams to mirrors also avoids the time constraint problem associated with a "pop-up" system. Nevertheless, this plan is also fraught with difficulties. Aside from the vulnerability of the orbiting mirrors to direct attack, accurate mirror function would be extremely sensitive to any physical aberrations. One ten-millionth of a meter of mirror distortion would cause appreciable decline in the performance of the excimer laser weapon. It would not take much to damage a mirror or disrupt its function. Even a one-ounce steel pellet moving at ten miles per second (the collision speed of two objects moving in opposite directions at orbiting speed in space) would penetrate six inches of steel.

Moreover, the effectiveness of any ground-based laser beam is substantially tempered by mirror reflection, atmospheric absorption of ultraviolet light, and changes in air density (e.g., cloud cover). One measure for counteracting ultraviolet light loss would be to increase the power supply to a level that approximates 20 percent to 60 percent of the entire electrical generating capacity of the U.S. "You cannot realistically supply that kind of power with anything other than some type of nuclear reactor system," claimed Air Force Col. George Hess, Strategic Defense Initiative Organization official. "Sooner or later, we're going to have to face the problem of public acceptance of the presence of nuclear reactors in space."

Another vulnerable characteristic of the "Star Wars" system is its dependence on computer software. The computer program must be able to identify, track, and destroy several thousand targets within 120 to 200 seconds without error the first time it is used. Statistically, however, undiscovered flaws will surface in every major computer program after being put into use. Computer equipment already in use for detecting incoming missiles has produced dozens of false alerts. Fortunately, as mentioned earlier, these errors were uncovered in time to forestall "retaliatory" attacks on an enemy. The fast-acting offensive and defensive weapons that "Star Wars" would encourage would permit little time to discern computer errors or false alerts before triggering a nuclear exchange.

To repeat: Even "Star Wars" proponents do not claim it can intercept all attackers. A 90 percent success could not prevent the destruction of our major population centers. Either nation intent on destroying the other could afford to lose most of its nuclear-tipped missiles and still have enough left over to accomplish its purpose. It has been estimated that only 2 percent of Soviet warheads could destroy 150 American cities.

Obviously, American military planners have to anticipate the nature of Soviet countermeasures to the "Star Wars" system. The effectiveness of "Star Wars" lasers could be reduced in a number of ways: By hardening the shells of the attacking missiles; by covering the booster with heat-absorbing layers; by spinning missiles in flight in order that the most vulnerable places will have an increased measure of protection; by redesigning the missiles to complete their boost phase inside the earth's atmosphere, immobilizing both X-ray lasers and particle beams, as they would scatter in the earth's atmosphere; or by using sporadic or asymmetrical booster flames to thwart location and tracking of a target spot on a ballistic missile. Another way of bypassing "Star Wars" interception is by using low-flying cruise missiles or manned bombers. Or large numbers of sophisticated decoys could saturate receptors and interceptors.

In order to meet the president's goal of replacing deterrence by retaliation with deterrence by defense, Paul Nitze, a senior arms control negotiator for the Reagan administration, has asserted that the "Star Wars" system must be able to survive a nuclear attack (operating at near 100 percent levels of effectiveness) and be cheaper to build than it would be for the Soviet Union to overcome. There is a general consensus among political experts and technocrats that it is much easier and less costly to circumvent or attack a defensive system than to produce a defensive system that continually requires upgrading. In their analysis of the ramifications of "Star Wars," Sidney D. Drell, Philip J. Farley, and David Holloway, of the Center for International Security and Arms Control at Stanford University, noted that for $5 million to $10 million apiece, the Soviets could buy a lot of warheads for defense penetration before equalling the 1981 Department of Defense estimate of $500 billion for deploying a space-based ballistic missile defense.

The widely accepted five-year cost estimates of $26 billion for "Star Wars" are little more than spontaneous educated guesses. Former Secretary of Defense James Schlesinger warned that a research program could not effectively absorb more than a 30 percent to 40 percent annual increase; yet the plan called for a 100 percent increase on funding for the second year. Norman Augustine, president of Martin Marietta Denver Aerospace, noted that defense R and D projects typically take one-third longer and cost one-third more than predicted at the outset. Given the complexity of the program, and considering the typical pattern of cost ratios between research and development and actual deployment of weapons, the Council on Economic Priorities estimated that the total cost would reach a minimum of $400 billion to $800 billion, if all went as planned. Proponents of "Star Wars" have not offered solutions to the budgetary dilemma this presents to American taxpayers faced with an existing trillion-dollar deficit incurred largely during the Reagan administration. A passage from an address by Gen. Douglas MacArthur in 1957 seems prophetic: "Our government has kept us in a perpetual state of fear—kept us in a continuous stampede of patriotic fervor—with the cry of grave national emergency . . . Always there has been some terrible evil to gobble us up if we did not blindly rally behind it by furnishing the exorbitant sums demanded. Yet, in retrospect, these disasters seem never to have happened, seem never to have been quite real."

The prohibitive costs combined with the adequacy and survivability problems of a system aimed at *total* defense have lent appeal to those who argue the utility of constructing a less-than-perfect defense. One of the leading advocates of "partial" defense is Fred S. Hoffman, whose study team analyzed the cost-effectiveness of "Star Wars" for the Pentagon. He maintains that a "partial" defense, aimed at limiting damage and protecting our nuclear arsenal, would be more readily achieved and would enhance the deterrent value of our nuclear weapons rather than ultimately replacing those missiles, as President Reagan has suggested. Testifying before the Senate Armed Services Committee, Hoffman argued that "defense of relatively moderate capability can make them [ballistic missiles] obsolete to a military planner long before they are important in terms of their indiscriminate destructive potential."

Other individuals, like George Keyworth, find the idea of replacing our nuclear arsenal debatable under any circumstances. "Do we want to abandon deterrence?" he asks. "Even though many critics may state that those of us who advocate strategic defense are calling for such a policy, there is no question that we must retain a specific retaliatory capability . . . Even if one were to have perfect defenses, an overt no-retaliation posture would have precisely the fatal fascination of the fortress that has proved disastrous throughout history." According to Lt. Gen. Brent Scowcroft, it is equally unrealistic to think that the Soviets could be convinced that it would be in their best interest to relinquish some of their strategic forces when those forces constitute their only means to penetrate the defense of the U.S.

There are two major problems with the strategy of a "partial" defense for enhancing our current nuclear deterrent. One is that each side would find it prudent to overestimate the power necessary to overcome the defenses of the other side—thus defeating the purpose of a partial defense system. Taken to the extreme, this scenario would result in all-out warfare to ensure a direct hit. The other is that the combination of a partial defense with stockpiled offensive weapons is bound to result in an increased temptation to strike first unless preceded by a dramatic reduction in offensive forces.

In a statement before the House Appropriations Committee, James Thomson of the RAND Corporation, a California-based think tank, explained that if both the United States and the Soviet Union were to add defenses to their offensive arsenal, the side to strike first would have the advantage because the limited retaliation could be absorbed by the defense system. Thomson concluded that the success of offensive arms reduction may be the sine qua non for a successful application of strategic defense. Paul Nitze, one of the most security-minded members of the Reagan administration, agreed that a defense with a reduced offensive arsenal would offer both sides "increased security at lower costs."

Former Secretary of Defense Harold Brown articulated the importance of arms reduction: "At least theoretically, sufficiently drastic and verifiable reductions in offensive forces could open up the possibility of a near-perfect defense. Arms control, in other words, could provide the means to achieve the same objective sought by proponents of SDI." Former Secretaries of Defense Robert S. McNamara and James R. Schlesinger stand in agreement with these assumptions.

It is only common sense to recognize that "Star Wars" runs counter to efforts to seek arms control agreements with the Soviet Union. The attempt to leapfrog into a supposed position of military superiority could effectively negate hopes for cutting back on the arms race. Indeed, it is possible that the Reagan administration anticipated this breakdown with its announcement that it would not feel bound by SALT II. Its publicly stated reason for doing so was that the Soviet Union was guilty of violations. Yet "Star Wars" itself runs directly counter to the Anti-Ballistic Missile Treaty. Article V of that Treaty states: "Each party undertakes not to develop, test, or deploy ABM systems or components which are sea-based, air-based, space-based, or mobile land-based." The president's 1985 Arms Control Impact statement concluded that lasers and other directed energy weapons, when in the field-testing phase, are also prohibited by the ABM Treaty. A Federation of American Scientists study showed that the "Star Wars" research and development program is at best borderline if not already violating ABM Treaty regulations. Due to the nature and scope of the proposed "Star Wars" project, it threatens to violate the Outer Space and Limited Test-Ban Treaties as well.

In early 1986, the ABM Treaty and the Limited Test-Ban Treaty were the only ratified treaties in the arms race between the two countries. Combined with SALT II, they have been something of a check on the arms race, although loosely drawn and, therefore, loosely interpreted. For example, the ABM Treaty does not permit "ABM systems or components." Our interpretation of the treaty prohibits completely functioning ABM units or isolated units capable of functioning in an ABM mode, yet allows us to test small parts applicable to ABM research. Neither has the Soviet Union neglected the loopholes in the treaty.

Research (which is impossible to verify) is allowed under the ABM Treaty. The Department of Defense has spent from $200 million to $1 billion per year on ballistic missile defense since the ABM Treaty was signed in 1972. The Soviet Union has deployed an ABM system around Moscow, which it claims is within the limits of the treaty. Regional nuclear threats (e.g., China and perhaps Pakistan) represent a rationale for the Soviet Union in deploying its "limited" ABM system. The Soviet Union has also installed a radar station near Krasnoyarsk, in Central Siberia—the size and positioning of which suggests that it could ultimately be part of an ABM system. Of all the alleged Soviet treaty violations, this one is most commonly agreed upon as verifiable.

In a radical departure from the practices of the Nixon, Ford, and Carter administrations, the Reagan administration chose a confrontational approach to arms control negotiations by publicizing allegations of Soviet treaty violations instead of resolving differences through normal diplomatic channels. The three previous U.S. presidents chose to bring such issues before the Standing Consultative Committee (SCC), a body established as the result of the SALT I agreements to resolve situational issues of compliance, attempting whenever possible to allay public fears about the success of compliance resolution. These three administrations were committed to maintaining arms control agreements on the premise that the Soviets would see that it was in their best interest to comply with the terms of the agreements and that undetected cheating on a scale large enough to alter the balance of power would be detectable in a very short time. Paul Warnke asserts, "If you figure you can't have arms control unless the Russians are nice guys, then it seems to me that you're being totally illogical. If the Russians could be trusted to be nice guys, you wouldn't need strategic arms control. And you wouldn't need strategic arms. Happy days would be here again. I think you have to start off with the premise that they are going to do a lot of things that are quite objectionable to us . . ."

"Star Wars" is publicly intended to counteract the arms increases by the Soviet Union since 1972. Overlooked is the fact that Soviet military weapons programs are completed ten to fifteen years after political decisions have been made. According to John Steinbruner, director, and Edward A. Hewett, Senior Fellow, of Foreign Policy Studies at the Brookings Institution, the Soviet increase in weapons inventories in the seventies was the result of planning done in the sixties—in response to the most massive build-up of U.S. arsenals ever undertaken in the history of the arms race. This example demonstrates one of the most obvious lessons in nuclear arms race history—that any action taken by one superpower to increase its military position will be met by an equal or greater reaction from the other.

The mirror-image in the military policies of both countries is the one feature that has persisted through all the combinations and permutations of the advances in military technology since the end of World War II. Despite the evidence that attempts to achieve a clear margin of military superiority are as fallacious as they are costly, both countries have allowed themselves to succumb to the persuasions of their scientists and military planners.

Although the quest for such superiority may be doomed to failure, it leads to tremendous power gains by certain segments of the society. In the Soviet Union, the military has long been engaged in a three-cornered battle for power and position with the Communist Party and the KGB The military competition with the United States provides the Soviet military with its most potent argument for increased budgets. In 1963, when I met with Premier Khrushchev on behalf of President John F. Kennedy, in an effort to clarify the American position on the nuclear Test-Ban Treaty, I was fascinated with the Russian leader's description of the constant pressure he was under from his military.

"Hardly a week passes without my generals coming to me with all sorts of terrifying stories—presented with all sorts of secret documents—saying that the Soviet Union is far behind the United States in the development of this or that weapon. They tell me that they cannot be responsible for the security of our country unless they get more rubles—billions of rubles—for protecting us against your schemes to get ahead of us. I know the same thing is happening in your country. The generals need each other. That is the best way they have of strengthening their positions and making themselves important."

When I reported to President Kennedy on this conversation with Premier Khrushchev, he smiled and nodded. "Khrushchev has the system down pat," he said. "I can tell the same story from this end, with this difference: when I ask the generals if they can assure me that they will really achieve the superiority they seek and will not come back asking for more, they shift in their seats and stammer. Of course, they can't assure us of anything except that they'll be back asking for more money—and the result is generally less security. I hope you told Khrushchev that there is no one in the Democratic Party or the Republican Party who is more genuinely eager than I am to negotiate seriously with the Soviet Union in putting an end to the widening spiral in which we are both trapped." Since the president had made a similar statement to me before I left for Moscow, I could answer that I was very diligent in delivering the message.

Robert S. McNamara and Nobel physicist Hans A. Bethe warned that "all our technological genius and economic prowess cannot make us secure if they leave the Soviet Union insecure." A classic case in point is the Multiple Independently Targeted Reentry Vehicle (MIRV)—multiple warheads carried by one missile capable of going to separate targets. The U.S. developed MIRVs in the 1960s to penetrate Soviet ABM defenses in case of a technological breakthrough and was unwilling to forgo the testing and deployment of MIRVs in order to retain a bargaining position for arms talks. However, during the 1979 SALT II negotiations, the Soviet Union refused to limit MIRVs so long as there was a large U.S. lead in this technology. The net result was the making of an agreement to constrain numbers of missiles—and not warheads. As expected, the

Soviet Union acquired the technology and deployed MIRVs fully into its ICBM force. The result was disadvantageous to the U.S. The Soviets could hang more MIRVs on their large ICBMs than the U.S. could on its smaller missiles.

The scientific imperative that seeks new technologies "lest the Soviets get the technology first" ignores the demonstrated reality that the Soviet Union can do anything we can do. For the Soviets to get the technology second could prove to be even more disadvantageous to us than if they were to get it first. Former National Security Adviser Robert McFarlane admitted, ". . . we may not have given proper attention to the strategic implications of weapons that cannot be easily detected, or of a world in which we or the Soviets may be able to deny the other information about our activities and capabilities."

If not curtailed, the cruise missile and F-15 anti-satellite (ASAT) weapons are two such weapons which would ultimately undermine our own security. The cruise missile, with its deadly nuclear cargo, eludes radar tracking by hugging the ground. It would remain undetected by a "Star Wars" system. The F-15 ASAT weapon is difficult to monitor because of its small size and varied launch locations. It could cripple military monitoring and control, adding to the incentive to strike first during crisis.

Fortunately, since 1982, the Soviets have observed a unilateral moratorium on ASAT testing. The strength of the American legislative system of checks and balances manifested itself in the House and Senate Subcommittee on Defense decision to ban future testing of ASATs—despite personal appeals from the president to the contrary —until it could be proved that the Soviets resumed testing of their ground-based ASAT system.

The Department of Defense and Department of State document entitled *Soviet Strategic Defense Programs* sums up the problem: "If the USSR in the future were unilaterally to add an effective advanced defense against ballistic missiles to its offensive and other defensive forces, it would pose a very serious new threat to U.S. and allied security." It should be no surprise that the Soviet Union has reacted to the prospect of "Star Wars" by the U.S. in almost identical terms as the U.S. reaction to the prospect of a significant increase in Soviet defensive capability.

The history of the arms race demonstrates that, with "Star Wars," arms reduction seems increasingly unlikely based on our anticipations of the Soviet response to a unilateral change in military policy and the ambiguous nature of defining the effectiveness of defense systems. Moreover, arms reduction may directly hinge on the "Star Wars" program. Soviet leader Mikhail Gorbachev proposed in 1986 a progressive elimination of all nuclear weapons by the year 2000, but indicated strongly that it may be contingent upon deferral of "Star Wars" for all the reasons we would have given had they proposed the same program.

In any event, all the questions over the merits or validity of the "Star Wars" system may miss the main point. The main point is that enough evidence has accumulated to show that a major rationale for "Star Wars" is that it can obtain hundreds of billions of dollars for military spending. Even if the Soviets could show that they have the technological capability to knock down our SDI stations in space or to put up their own, the SDI advocates would press forward. A trillion-dollar budget has a life of its own.

Not the least disturbing aspect of the seemingly headlong policy to put limitless sums into "Star Wars" is the evidence that money for congressional lobbying has come out of overcharging. For example, in August 1986, the Air Force admitted that Lockheed had overcharged by more than a half-billion dollars in government orders. Meanwhile, the U.S. General Accounting Office has reported instances in which arms contractors, including Lockheed, had spent large sums to influence government policy.

Two accidents occurring early in 1986 have a great deal to teach us about the vulnerability of modern society to high technology. One is the explosion of the U.S. space shuttle *Challenger*. The other is the disaster at the Chernobyl nuclear power plant near Kiev in the Ukraine, in the Soviet Union.

Mention was made earlier of the integral role of computers in "Star Wars" technology. Begin with the computerized system for detecting attacking missiles. During World War II, civilian spotters would stand on hilltops of American coastal cities and report the sight or sound of airplanes by telephone to a control station. These reports would be checked against information at hand about posted flights. Unidentified aircraft would be monitored on a grid from station to station. At the beginning of the war, most military aircraft flew at speeds under 400 miles per hour; many of them under 200 m.p.h. There was ample time for the tracking station to check and cross-check all movements in the sky in time to transmit an alert to our own combat aircraft as well as to activate anti-aircraft equipment. Before the end of the war, however, speeds of aircraft had increased to the point where civilian spotters were as useless as Indian smoke signals against an attacker with field cannons. Radar replaced surveillance by human eyes. Within a few years, military jets were flying faster than the speed of sound. Then came ballistic missiles, with speeds measured not in terms of hundreds of miles per hour but thousands of miles per hour. Even enemies on opposite sides of the world were only two or three hours apart.

As the speed of missiles increased, so did reliance on technology. By the mid-1970s, computers were given the job of analyzing data appearing on radar screens from our tracking stations around the world. Complete logs were kept of authorized maneuvers of aircraft. The presence of unauthorized or strange objects would be picked up by our radar stations and fed into computers which had the capability of determining whether such objects had any significance in terms of possible attacking missiles or planes. We then would have an hour or two to activate our defenses or our retaliatory missiles.

In the years from 1981 to 1985, more than a hundred possible missile attacks on the United States were flashed on our military computer screens. Fortunately, we had enough time to check out these alerts and determine that they were the result of computer error. It might take as much as fifteen minutes or a half hour to discover that a signal was false. But at least we had that margin of time to prevent buttons from being pressed that would turn loose a nuclear attack on the enemy, resulting, in all probability, in a counter nuclear attack on the United States.

There being no reason to believe that Soviet computer technology is superior to our own, it becomes necessary to recognize the fact that erroneous blips have turned up on Soviet computer screens. But America's very success in placing missile launching platforms close to the borders of the Soviet Union has reduced the time available to Soviet experts for checking the computers for possible errors. For example, American Pershing 2 missiles are less than ten minutes away from major Soviet targets. Since this may not provide enough time to rule out the possibility of computer error, Soviet decision-makers may have to bet the life of their nation on a guess as to technology performance. This puts not just the Soviet and American peoples but the world's people in jeopardy because of computer error or malfunction.

The fact of Soviet submarines with missile launchers not far off the coasts of the United States has a similar effect on American defense strategy—so much so, in fact, that serious discussions have been held inside the government as to whether we should turn loose our nuclear retaliatory capability on alert rather than on verification, since there may not be enough time for the latter.

Perhaps the most basic flaw of all in the computer alert system is that it doesn't allow for third-party complicity. The computer can, of course, tell something from the shape and a great deal from the early location of a blip on a radar screen, but not all blips are picked up at site of origin. The precise source of a possible attack on the U.S. can be something of a guessing game. A missile launched by a submarine, for example, provides no automatic or certain information about the identity of the sender. A third party that thinks it is in a position to profit from a war between two other nations could conceivably launch its missile at one or the other, thus setting off a nuclear chain reaction.

Theoretically, the hot line between the United States and the Soviet Union is designed to guard against such a possibility. But the absurdity of this approach is made dramatic by the fact that the United States has spent hundreds of billions of dollars to defend against the possibility of a surprise attack. The underlying assumption here is that a surprise attack is indeed not just a realistic possibility but the most likely scenario in the event that an enemy should decide to go to war against us. One can readily imagine the "Alice in Wonderland" quality of a telephone call that is made in expectation of learning the truth, if indeed, the party at the other end of the telephone actually launched the attack.

Still another risk is represented by measures set up to ensure our retaliatory ability. American defense planners have had to take into account the danger of a surprise attack on our capital—an attack which conceivably could cost the lives of the president, vice-president, the chiefs of staff, and other high-ranking military officials. Indeed, a contingency plan has been put into effect under which it is assumed that the men in charge of our missile silos in the Midwest and Southwest might have to activate the retaliatory attack on an enemy even without specific orders. Elaborate precautions, of course, have been built into the system to protect against irresponsible individual preemption of decision making. Each member of the four-man team attached to a silo has a quarter of the key that is required to activate the missile. Even if one man should go berserk and take it into his head to dispatch a missile, the other three members of the team would stand in the way. Unfortunately, the system is not foolproof. It doesn't protect against the possibility of a conspiracy of all four members, or of one or more members of the team overwhelming the remaining members in order to carry out their design.

What is most likely, however, is that nuclear war could erupt without anyone having a clear idea of what went wrong. Human scientific genius has created the ultimate irrational situation in which the conditions of life could be shattered beyond recognition or repair, with the survivors, such as they are, left to guess how it all started.

What is to be learned from the space shuttle disaster is that the entire human race is in a spaceship and the decision-making time for correcting mistakes has been cut to seconds. The men at the controls have become so preoccupied with staying ahead in the arms race that they are neglecting the painstaking joint attention required to keep the spaceship on course.

The accident at Chernobyl, like earlier accidents at the Three-

Mile Island plant in the United States on March 28, 1979, and at Windscale Pile in England on October 7, 1957, involved a combination of human and mechanical error and demonstrated the validity of the principle that, whenever error is possible, error becomes inevitable at one time or another. The Chernobyl accident was believed to have been the result of a hidden loss of coolant, resulting in soaring temperatures in the reactor, which produced an explosion. Blocks of graphite encasing the uranium fuel, for the purpose of slowing the speed of neutrons emitted by the fuel, were exposed to air and caught fire because of the high temperatures. Graphite, like coal, has a high density and is long burning. Uranium pellets, damaged by the heat, figured in the venting of radioactive products of the fission process. The radioactive clouds that circled the world, producing measurable fallout on crops as well as universal alarm, were only a fraction of the atmospheric problems that would be caused by the explosion of nuclear bombs, sucking up thousands of tons of radioactive debris. Atomic scientists have made careful calculations of the ratio between destructive force and the possibility of a cloud cover that would obscure the sun for many months, robbing the earth of the interaction of vital factors that support life and vegetation.

What is most instructive about Chernobyl is that, in our age, human error in any one place can jeopardize human beings everywhere. Thought patterns are national; the effects are global.

With the introduction of "Star Wars," space has become a focal point for global discussion—for space knows no geographic boundaries and orbiting weapons will circulate over warring and peaceful nations alike. Mankind's ability to create and use the means of its own extinction is the most pressing problem before the human race. It is a global problem and requires a global solution.

12

Two Kinds
of Sovereignty

I n a curious sense, the advent of total power has pushed the entire
human race back to the time when men were at the mercy of
bullies; that is, a time when government either did not exist or
was incapable of dealing with lawlessness. Today, the dominant
condition of mankind has reverted to anarchy. Whatever the present
forms of law and order in the world may be today, they have only
limited validity. For these forms exist only inside the nation. The
overriding danger to life in our time comes from the interactions of
nations in the world arena. In the absence of a higher tribunal, a
nation interprets for itself the requirements of justice. It inevitably
pursues its own self-interest in contact with other nations. And a
nation knows no law except self-determination. But the self-determination of one nation is the anarchy of all. And the ultimate consequences of world anarchy for the individual are even more menacing
than they would be inside the nation itself. The end product of world
anarchy could mean the end of the age of the human species.

The individual in today's world, therefore, can no longer look to
the nation as the main source of his security. For the nation is unable
to protect him against invasion or assault from other nations. Nor
is it able to guarantee the main conditions of his growth or to
safeguard his values or institutions or culture or property. No matter
how wide the oceans that surround the nation, no matter how bristling its defenses, its people have suddenly become vulnerable to

shattering attack. The nation possesses retaliatory power, true, but even in the exercise of that power it engages in a form of self-assault, for power today has its effects against the delicate and precarious conditions that make existence possible.

This is the central, overwhelming fact not just about national power but about national powerlessness in the twentieth century. The fully sovereign nation has become separated from its historic reason for being. It is not only incapable of protecting the lives, values, and property of its citizens; it has actually become inimical to life and creative freedom. It is inimical because it functions contrary to natural rights. Natural rights are above the rights of the state. Historically, the purpose of the good society, at least as defined by Jefferson, Adams, Franklin, and Madison, is to serve and protect these natural rights. The right of the individual to keep himself from being cheapened, debased, or deformed. The right to creative growth. The right to individual sanctity and sovereignty. The right to seek purpose in life. If these natural rights should die, though human flesh in some form remain, then the survivors will not be the lucky ones.

The state, too, has its rights; for example, the right to sacrifice human life or to take human life in the defense of the nation. But there is nothing in the political rights of the state or its rulers that includes the right to strike at the conditions of life itself. Nuclear war is not just a confrontation of national enemies. It is a war against the vital balances of nature that make life possible.

All sorts of "quick fixes" have been proposed for remedying the relationship between the U.S. and USSR But what is needed is not just a better manner or tone in the discourse between the two countries, useful though such improved approaches may be. What is needed is a structure of effective world organization into which both countries can fit. Thus, what counts is not just what each says to the other, but how, speaking and acting together, both countries propose to organize a durable peace. Our very clear mutual and ultimate aim should be not just to abolish nuclear weapons but to abolish war itself. Obviously, putting an end to the arms race is where we have to begin, but that is not where it ends. The arms race is the product of tensions even as it creates tensions. At some point, it will be necessary to think about the sources of world tensions and about scientific and structural approaches to the making of genuine peace.

What is most amazing about our world is that we have not really addressed ourselves to the structural requirements of world organization. The general idea behind the UN at its inception was that a code could be created for the conduct of nations beyond their own borders. This has yet to happen. Instead, the prevailing philosophy seems to be that the United Nations can only be a reflection of the world as it is. As has been evident for almost half a century, the world as it is is not good enough. A way must be found to transcend the world as it is. It is necessary to create machinery that can deal adequately with breakdowns among nations.

The U.S. and USSR have been overly fascinated with each other, almost to the point of mutual narcissism. They have assumed that, if they could just resolve the problems involved in their own confrontation, the rest would fall into place. Certainly, everything possible should be done to resolve mutual problems, but what is clearly needed is a combined approach to world dangers. The two nations have become competitive in talking to the rest of the world but that is not what the world is waiting to hear. What the world is waiting to hear is what they are prepared to do, working together, to meet specific problems on a global level—the problems not just of sponsored terrorism but of world hunger, world environmental contamination, regional conflicts, social justice. It is quite possible that, if the two superpowers can just shift their gaze from each other to the need to make the planet safe and fit for human habitation, they may promote their own security even as they advance the common security.

When nations live in anarchy, the individual citizen pays the price. Law and order within the state are no protection against the larger violence and injustice outside the state. Whatever the intermediate forms of protection afforded individual citizens in their daily life, the major threats to their well-being find them open and exposed.

If this is what total sovereignty has come to mean, then it is a monstrous thing and human beings have the duty to create sane and workable institutions that conflict neither with nature itself nor with natural rights.

Just as absolute sovereignty today is incapable of producing peace, so it is incapable of ensuring freedom. To the extent that a nation looks to its own absolute sovereignty to achieve security and maintain freedom, it weakens both. In short, the absolute sovereign state is an inadequate shelter for human beings in a world of absolute power.

No matter how hard one sovereign state may try to pursue security through power, the power is never quite enough. For other states are increasing their power too. The state and its people are thus trapped in their own sovereign coils. To be without power when other nations are becoming powerful could be an invitation to attack and disaster. But the pursuit of power means the pursuit of superior power, hard to define and even harder to create.

The dilemma is especially acute for free peoples. They have been vulnerable to aggressors in the past precisely because their freeness makes for openness. And, even as they accept the need to become brawny in the cause of self-preservation, they become involved in something beyond their control—a massive competition in potential terror the very nature of which pulls them inexorably toward a showdown.

For the dictator state, the world condition of tension and uncertainty offers a natural habitat. The presence or prospect of an outer threat lends weight to the internal controls. But even if the dictator state is willing to modify its ideological ambitions, the mountain of its sovereign statehood still stands. The sovereignty precedes the ideology and indeed survives it. And in its sovereign role the dictator state may make concessions, it may permit deviations, but it will not surrender its position above the law. It insists on the unlimited and unfettered development and mobilization of its own power.

How, then, is the wall of unfettered sovereignty to be broken? If the free state is reluctant to accept higher controls, and the unfree state is adamant against those controls, where do we look for safety and sanity?

It becomes necessary, then, for the nation to develop new means of performing its historic role. If the existence of power can no longer serve as the main source of a nation's security, something else will have to take its place if human society is to be able to endure and function.

As with an individual or group confronted by the bully, the need is for enough people to come together to determine how to protect themselves in the light of existing conditions, and how to establish whatever new approaches or agencies may be required for the common safety. The new power that must be brought into being is power in its most natural form. It is the power represented by human will —the power of consensus. Out of it can come the energy and momentum for building a new flooring for human society. Out of it, too, can come workable checks on heretofore uncontrolled power—all as part of a system of justice in the intercourse of nations.

This leads to a paradox. The individual wants to create something beyond the nation that can give him the protections once afforded by the nation; yet the nation itself is his only instrumentality for achieving it. The only place an individual can find firm footing for a stand is inside a nation; how, therefore, can he be effective outside the nation?

Just as there is a concept of natural law that transcends the state, so there is a concept of natural will that can transcend the nation. A new force that is emerging in the world is the force of world public opinion. It is as yet without formal channels or organs of expression. No matter; it is a developing new power and it is becoming increasingly audible. Public opinion inside the nation is at its most powerful when it is concerned with questions of justice or overriding moral issues. Similarly, world public opinion can make its power felt on the big questions that have moral content or that are concerned with the rational means of safeguarding human life.

No freedom is more meaningful for the individual of a free society than to use that freedom in a cause that is not confined to the nation. He can use his footing inside the nation to work for a consensus inside the nation, one that can lead to effective commitments by the nation to an ordered society.

Do these commitments mean the end of national sovereignty?

No; they need mean only the end of *absolute* national sovereignty.

For there are two kinds of sovereignty. One is absolute. The other is relative.

Absolute sovereignty means that a nation will not submit itself to the *compulsory* jurisdiction of a world body in matters concerned with world disputes or problems; will not subordinate its military policy to a world body; will not agree in advance to a set of rules for world law under which its only recourse is a world court. In short, absolute sovereignty means that a state may be willing to negotiate on a treaty basis, but insists on the right of revocation as circumstances may warrant.

Relative sovereignty means that a state can retain jurisdiction over its way of life. The force available to it can be ample for purposes of internal security and development, but not for external aggression or conquest. The nature of nuclear weapons makes it possible to draw a line between the two. A nation does not need nuclear weapons to maintain law and order among its citizens, or even to deal with the threat of armed insurrection. Weapons adapted to mass destruction can therefore be removed from the jurisdiction of the nation and placed under the control of the world organization.

In a world without absolute national sovereignty, the world organization can underwrite national independence and relative sovereignty. It is not necessary for the nation to be dissolved in order to create a situation of safety on earth. It is necessary only for national sovereignty to be made meaningful, to eliminate those attributes of it that add up to world anarchy, and to assure and underwrite those attributes that add up to national responsibility.

We are living, all of us—whether Americans, Soviets, English, French, Chinese, Lebanese, Egyptians, or Siamese—in two totally different worlds.

The first of these worlds is old, familiar, visible, combustible, and unworkable. It is the world in which nations act as nations have always acted. Experience has taught that life is full of sneak attacks and that everything nations own may suddenly be taken from them. Hence, they attempt to achieve security through strength. It is natural that a nation should act to protect its self-interest in a world of conflicting national interests—a world in which the struggle for power is real and in which force has been used repeatedly to assert the national will.

The question of morality in such a world is irrelevant because morality cannot exist where a perpetual clash of interests is assumed and where brute force determines the ultimate shape of history.

Now we come to the second world. It is new, complex, exacting, difficult; it is also at once dangerous and promising. The second world is one of almost total change. It has changed the physical earth in its relationship to man. Vast distances have ceased to exist. The new reach and power of human beings know almost no tangible limits. Most important of all is that nuclear switches can now be pulled and whole nations and their peoples expunged from the face of the earth. There is also the prospect of an ultimate switch, soon to be created if it does not already exist, that can burn all life off the planet.

Such a new world imposes stern conditions. It requires a high order of intelligence. It cannot be subjected to unlimited strains or tensions. It will not operate itself. It must be operated; but the people who operate it must know what they are doing. In this sense it is as exacting and demanding and difficult as the highest science.

The principal stress point in such a world is absolute national sovereignty. And it is at this point that the two worlds, old and new, come into conflict. However logical and natural it may seem to a nation to assert its sovereignty through force or a show of force inside the old world of plot-and-counterplot, self-interest, and balance of power, the changed conditions of the new world make absolute national sovereignty unworkable. Military victory, the supreme achievement of sovereignty in the past, is no longer possible. Nations no longer declare war or wage war; they declare or wage mutual suicide.

The kind of action, therefore, that only a few years ago would have seemed proper and inevitable for a nation to take in pursuit of its self-interest no longer makes sense. Indeed, it can be the quickest way of putting a nuclear match to the planet.

We exist in two different worlds but we pay a price for it. Decisions may be made on the level of old-world thinking but the consequences take place in the new. A nation that is guided primarily by traditional ideas of self-interest may quickly discover it will lose its principal power. For workable power in the new world is measured by the leadership a nation is able to exert among the large majority of the peoples on earth, by its moral standing, by its ability to recognize new realities, by its desire not to use force but to control it.

Living in this new world does not mean we ignore the existence of threatening ideologies. It simply means we have to fashion new ways of competing with those ideologies. For Americans and Soviets, it means they can challenge each other to the most important competition of all—a competition in service to the human community. It is possible that victory is to be found on this level and on none other. Since raw force defeats it own purpose, it becomes necessary to develop the new approaches and ideas that happen to fit the new age. If Americans are seriously concerned about the threat of communism in the world, they will invest themselves and their resources in a total commitment to the cause of a better and safer world. They won't store or destroy their surplus wheat but use it in the war against hunger. They won't grumble about the veto in the UN, which they themselves sponsored, but will proclaim their readiness to be part of a UN with responsible, just, and effective authority. They won't attempt to improvise a police force for the UN on an emergency basis on matters affecting their national interests, but will advocate the need for a permanent UN force—adequate to deter aggression, adequate to carry out inspection as part of workable control over nuclear arms, adequate to keep the peace itself. And they will seek to codify the circumstances or situations in which police powers may be used, in order to guard against capricious or irresponsible use of such force. They will create the machinery of due process in order that justice may be primary in the resolution of disputes. In short, they will be concerned about the architecture, and not just the concept, of world peace under law.

These are some of the basic requirements imposed by the new world. An individual citizen of a nation does not serve the cause of his country just by cheering for his side every time it sends men with guns into other countries in an effort to protect its self-interest. For ultimate security depends not so much on the give-and-take of conflicting national self-interests as it does on a workable design for world peace. The clear aim must be to create a situation of sanity and safety in the world. This may enable the individual to be secure in the only way it is possible to be secure.

13

Purpose as Power

In the course of history, three great struggles have dominated human imagination and purpose.

The first has been for safety against the elements and for subsistence.

The second has been for freedom and growth.

The third has been for protection against war.

Great gains have been recorded in these struggles.

The battle against heat, cold, water, sand, and ice is no longer a dominant preoccupation of man as a whole. Theoretically it is at least now possible to develop the world's resources to the point where the human population will have enough to eat. Theoretically, too, it is at least now possible to develop enough energy to bring the central benefits of an industrial civilization to most of the world's peoples.

The battle for freedom has not yet been won; it may never be won. But at least the foundations of freedom have been laid and the principles established for many millions of the earth's population. The cause of freedom, however, is jeopardized in our time not only by those who are working for authoritarianism of one color or another but by a breakdown in human organization. For freedom cannot exist without law, just as law cannot exist without government; and the world as a whole today is still in a primitive, pregovernment form.

The third struggle—for protection against war—has been the only one of man's struggles in which he has known mounting defeat. In no other field of human enterprise has progress been as essential as in this; in no other field has the absence of progress been more marked or costly. The failure has grown from the earliest times, when the individual was totally without the protection of society or group, to the point when human society is completely vulnerable and unprotected.

There has never been any great difficulty in killing a person. Given the intent, the means were relatively simple. But society always did its best to interpose itself between the killer and the intended victim. It would outlaw concealed weapons; it would establish drastic punishments as deterrents; it would direct many of its efforts and facilities toward safeguarding a person against the predatoriness, the rapacity, and violence of his neighbors. Religions would lend their full force to the moral injunctions against violence.

These protections are now virtually meaningless alongside the utter ease with which society itself can put an end to life. None of its skills, indeed, have been more highly developed than this. To be able to put death into the air without changing the odor or the texture of the air; to be able to create invisible bullets that pierce skin and bone and rip open human chromosomes and genes; to be able to devise lethal droplets, any one of which can terminate life in brief contact with the human skin; to be able to tamper with the precarious balances through which nature serves all life; to be able to twist a person's character all out of shape and control his thoughts—these skills are all now claimed by human intelligence in the name of national security.

Man today is not safe in the presence of man. The old cannibalism has given way to anonymous action in which the killer and the killed do not know each other, and in which, indeed, the very fact of mass death has the effect of making the killing less reprehensible than the death of a single man.

In short, man has evolved in every respect except his ability to protect himself against human intelligence. His knowledge is vast but does not embrace the workings of peace. Because he attaches importance to a rounded view of life, he studies history, philosophy, religions, languages, literature, art, architecture, and political science. Because he is concerned about his well-being, he studies anthropology, biology, medicine, psychology, and space. Because he is interested in technical progress, he studies chemistry, physics, engineering, mathematics, and sanitation. But he has yet to make peace basic in his education. The most important subject in this world is hardly taught at all. The basic principles involved in creating a situation of safety; the effective limits of national sovereignty; the fundamental elements that must go into the making of world law—unless these are pursued and understood, nothing else he knows will do him any good.

All people—whether they go by the name of Americans or Soviets or Chinese or British or Indians or Africans—have obligations to one another that transcend their obligations to their sovereign societies. For the conflicts that involve twentieth-century man are not solely ideological or political. They are personal, historic, transcendent. They involve his relationship to others all the way from the immediate community that surrounds him to the human commonwealth as a whole.

These conflicts can be resolved in terms of first principles:

• If there is a conflict between the security of the sovereign state and the security of the human commonwealth, the human commonwealth comes first.

• If there is a conflict between the well-being of the nation and the well-being of mankind, the well-being of mankind comes first.

• If there is a conflict between the needs of this generation and the needs of all the later generations, the needs of the later generations come first.

• If there is a conflict between the rights of the state and the rights of man, the rights of man come first. The state justifies its existence only as it serves and safeguards the rights of man.

• If there is a conflict between public edict and private conscience, private conscience comes first.

• If there is a conflict between the easy drift of prosperity and the ordeal of peace, the ordeal of peace comes first.

With these first principles in operation, the people can create a mandate for government. Such a mandate would enable the nation to put first things first. The nation can declare that, even in its self-defense, it will not engage in a war that would destroy the rest of the world. Neither will it hesitate to declare that it would rather die than be the first to use chemical, biological, or nuclear weapons on human beings.

It could declare that it considers it a privilege to commit and dedicate everything it has—its resources, energy, knowledge, and moral imagination—to the making of a genuine peace under justice and law through the development of world institutions adequate to meet common dangers and common needs.

The nation in today's world is confronted with the same principal dangers it has had to face throughout history—represented mainly by unstable or predatory or aggressive neighbors. But the traditional forces of protection are no longer workable. Military force is still the main reliance against aggression, but the nature of that force today contains built-in hazards and contradictions. Atomic explosives are tied to the assumption that a foe places higher value on his life than you do on yours. A psychological factor is at work in which it is assumed that the enemy will be guided by a rational consideration, i.e., the supreme importance of his own survival. Yet this consideration is contradicted by the proclaimed readiness to use weapons that are also self-annihilating.

And even without respect to use, the political and economic forces generated by the manufacture of the weapons can disfigure a society.

The challenge, therefore, is to recognize that national security depends on a wide range of factors, some of them nonmilitary in nature. The freedoms, well-being, and strength of the society itself; acceptance of the principle that the highest resources of the nation are represented by the fullest possible development of the potentialities of its citizens; the presence of knowledgeable and creative leadership at the top, steering the nation through complex, day-by-day situations at home and abroad; the articulation of goals that impart energy to a people that gain the respect and support of other peoples; helping to strengthen world institutions for meeting world problems; the recognition that nations themselves have to be governed for the common good—all these are connected to genuine national and collective safety.

Human purpose connected to these challenges provides antidotes to the pathology of power. Indeed, human purpose may be the greatest power of all.

Postscript

The central theme in this book is the way power in government becomes enlarged, exploited, and institutionalized, not just as the result of external dangers, real or contrived, but as the result of the way the arms race spills over into and dominates foreign policy. The power is not easily controlled, nor are the effects readily contained. At the point where the power spills over into areas where it becomes a visible and dramatic threat, it can be challenged by press and public. The resulting disruptions and dislocations, however, are apt to be damaging to the position of the nation in the world.

A prime example of this problem surfaced in the closing months of 1986. The surreptitious sale of arms to Iran, coincident with the release of an American-held hostage, was disclosed by a foreign newspaper and was widely interpreted as a repudiation by President Ronald Reagan of his stated policy against negotiating with terrorists. The clamor over this event became compounded when it was revealed that funds from the arms transaction had been secretly passed through to government opposition forces in Nicaragua, thus putting the Administration in the position of tapping the nation's funds outside the constitutional process. It also developed that the merchants of death were applying their pressures on government, not just from the outside but from the inside.

At first, President Reagan made three attempts to explain the situation to the satisfaction of the American people—but the result each time was increased public confusion and vexation. It now appears that some of the new merchants of death can be found within the American government itself, men who are ready to sell arms and munitions heedless of the fact that these very weapons may be trained on nations friendly to the United States or even used against our own soldiers. Finally, the major issue emerging from the entire affair concerned the right of the American people to full information concerning their vital interests as a free people. The incontestable and towering fact about the episode was that the American people had to push and prod to get at the truth.

Truth may be an esoteric language, but it is the only language the U.S. government is authorized by its history to speak to its people. Americans need not be grateful for being told the truth by their government; this is their natural right.

In recent years, however, a strange new notion has gained ground. It is the idea that the government has options with respect to truth. A possible beginning date for this departure is 1947 with an act setting up the Central Intelligence Agency. That act authorized the government to practice secret violence, deceit, and subversion as essential parts of the conduct of U.S. foreign policy, but specifically confined such undercover actions to foreign territory.

The justification for those actions was that we were living in a hard, predatory, cloak-and-dagger world and that the only way to deal with a totalitarian enemy was to imitate him.

The trouble with this theory was that, while we live in a world of plot and counterplot, we also live in a world of cause and effect. Whatever the cause for the decision to legitimize and regularize deceit abroad, the inevitable effect was the practice of deceit at home. Long before the Iranian episode and secret funding of the Contras, the government was doing one thing and saying another. In 1959, for example, the United States was secretly involved in an attempted coup against Laos. When the central role of the U.S. in the coup was exposed, there were denials all around. But the evidence mounted and the actual facts couldn't be suppressed.

Another example. In 1971, President Nixon declared that no military operations had been conducted against Cambodia. Pentagon officials testified to the same effect before a Congressional committee. It was later established that more than 3,000 bombing operations had been carried out against Cambodia.

The main danger in these and other episodes is represented not just by the break with truth but by the things we did that we had to deny. If truth is to mean anything, it must be a total process, including policies and actions of government that require neither concealment nor later denials or apologies.

The fatal defect in the 1947 act authorizing dirty tricks is clear: An integral part of dirty tricks is the cover-up. Since the U.S. government is prohibited from lying to the American people under this act, how is the cover-up to be compartmentalized so that people abroad are fooled but people at home are "in the know"? This raises an equally important question: Why is it all right to lie to foreigners? Wherefore the assumption that moral issues cease at the water's edge? Two hundred years ago, the young men who founded the United States proclaimed a "decent regard for the opinions of mankind." The term "unAmerican activities" should apply in its most fundamental sense to a double-standard which permits one standard abroad and proscribes another at home.

Truth by government will not assert itself. It has to be institutionalized. Truth needs a form of its own that transcends the men who happen to be in charge of the machinery of government at any given moment. This is what is meant by a government of laws rather than of men. This is what the main design produced by the Philadelphia Constitutional Convention of 1787 was all about. But this design has been slipping away from us in recent years. We have permitted exceptions from principle in the operation of our society, exceptions that should not be accommodated or metabolized. We have made it possible for men in government to become bigger than the laws they have sworn to uphold.

Governments are not built to perceive large truths. Only people can perceive great truths. Governments specialize in small and intermediate truths. They have to be instructed by their people in great truths. And the particular truth in which they need instruction today is that new means for meeting the largest problems on earth have to be created. Individual nations can unleash wars but are incapable individually of preventing them.

It will be said that our style in the international arena is dictated by others, and that we have no choice but to play the game according to the way others play it. Yet it is precisely because we have to take the world as it is that becomes necessary to rise above the game if we wish to make our mark. We cannot expect to succeed in the world political arena by being more volatile than anyone else in the game of combustible anarchy. We will succeed only as we represent a rallying center in the world for a less hazardous and more sensible future for all people than is now apparent. Our energies will have a far greater effect if we apply them to the possibilities for human progress rather than to shadowy balance-of-power strategies.

It is not reasonable or logical to assume that national statesmen will lead the way in the taming of nations or in the rebuilding of the United Nations. Do not expect, Alexander Hamilton wrote, nations to take the initiative in developing restraints upon themselves. An essential truth that has to be recognized is that no rational process now exists for assuring the basic safety of the human species. We stumble into the future day to day, dependent for our survival more on the hope that our margin for error may not have been completely exhausted than on a working design for a peaceful world.

If we want truth to live a less unnatural and precarious existence than at present, we will make world law the central and open objective of our foreign policy. Any nation that comes forward with such an aim can expect to be rebuffed. But there is a distinction between rebuff and defeat. There is no defeat for the American people when they tie themselves to the great idea that human intelligence is equal to human needs. Beyond the clamor of clashing ideologies and the preening and jostling of sovereign tribes, a safer and more responsible world is waiting to be created.

Notes

CHAPTER 2 *The Misperception of Power*

Quotations on pages 2–11 from messages, decisions, and conversations among the Joint Chiefs, commanders in the field, diplomats, the President, and other parties consulted, are taken from the Defense Department publication *The Entry of the Soviet Union into the War Against Japan: Military Plans: 1941–1945.* This detailed account includes the plans rejected or accepted, and other data giving immediacy to the decisions of the war years.

The specific issue of whether the war against Japan could have been ended without the use of the atomic bomb has been explored in a number of studies in England and the United States. Perhaps the most comprehensive of these works is *Atomic Diplomacy: Hiroshima and Potsdam, the Use of the Atomic Bomb and the American Confrontation with Soviet Power,* by Gar Alperovitz. The quotation from General Hap Arnold is taken from this book, p. 17. The quote from Truman's diary in regard to his conversation with Stalin is taken from *Off the Record; The Private Papers of Harry S. Truman,* edited by Robert H. Ferrell. Other quotations from Truman are taken from the same book. The *U.S. News and World Report* interviews are from an August 15, 1960, article entitled "Was A-Bomb a Mistake?" The quotations from Admiral Leahy are from his book *I Was There: The Personal Story of the Chief of Staff to Presidents Roosevelt and Truman, Based on His Notes and Diaries Made at the Time,* pages 439–42. Teller's preference for first use of the bomb on a noncivilian target is referred to in Peter Wyden's book *Day One: Before Hiroshima and After,* p. 175. President Eisenhower's response on hearing at Potsdam of the successful testing of the atomic bomb is referred to in *Crusade in Europe,* p. 443 and discussed again in his later book *Mandate for Change,* pp. 312–13. The U.S. Strategic

Bombing Survey, conducted in the summer of 1945, published its assessment of Japan's military capabilities in July 1946, in a report entitled "Japan's Struggle to End the War." The quotation cited in this chapter is from p. 13 of the report.

CHAPTER 4 *General MacArthur in Fact and Fiction*

A report of the author's conversation with General MacArthur first appeared in *The Saturday Review,* May 2, 1964. General MacArthur's address to the American Legion on January 26, 1955, and his message to the Mayor of Hiroshima of August 6, 1947, appear in Vorin E. Wahn, Jr.'s book, *A Soldier Speaks.*

CHAPTER 6 *Unremembered History*

As indicated in the text, extensive quotations in this chapter come from *The Merchants of Death,* by H. C. Engelbrecht and F. C. Hanighen, and *The Private Manufacture of Arms,* by Nobel Peace Prize winner Philip Noel-Baker. Senator Humphrey's observation is taken from Michael Klare's book *American Arms Supermarket,* p. 2. The State Department official was quoted in an article in the *Wall Street Journal,* June 29, 1983, and in Klare's book on p. 1.

CHAPTER 7 *The Whistle-Blowers*

Quotations regarding the findings of La Rocque's task force on the Vietnam War are from the June 1981 issue of *Playboy* magazine, p. 139, as excerpted and reprinted by the Center of Defense Information. The reference to President Nixon's use of *The Defense Monitor* is from an article in the *Air Force Times,* which appeared on January 26, 1976. The quotation from the Joint Committee on Defense Production is taken from a November 26, 1976, article in *The Des Moines Register.* La Rocque's concerns are further explained in Studs Terkel's book *The Good War* and articles in *The Christian Science Monitor* (October 30, 1984), *The Washingtonian* (January 1973, pp. 35–37, 40), and the *Wall Street Journal* (April 24, 1972).

Cost-overrun findings are described in Ernest Fitzgerald's articles for *World* Magazine (February 27, 1973) and in Dina Rasor's book *More Bucks, Less Bang: How the Pentagon Buys Ineffective Weapons.* The quotation regarding Fitzgerald's First Law of Program Management is also from his article in *More Bucks*. His statement about suing for work appeared in an article about him in the December 9, 1985, issue of *People* magazine, pp. 77–83. The information in this chapter on Dina Rasor came from her own books, *The Pentagon Underground* and *More Bucks*.

CHAPTER 8 *The Gold-Tipped Iceberg*

Information about the House of Representatives investigation into arms contracts was obtained from "Review of Allowable Costs in Overhead Submission of Defense Contractors," the report of joint hearings held by the House of Representatives Armed Services Committee subcommittee on Seapower and Strategic and Critical Materials and the House subcommittee on Investigations. Articles by William Boly, James Fallows, and Knut Royce, which originally appeared in other publications, are drawn together by Dina Rasor in *More Bucks, Less Bang: How the Pentagon Buys Ineffective Weapons*. The report of the House Armed Services investigating subcommittee headed by Representative Richard Ichord is also summarized in *More Bucks*.

CHAPTER 9 *Weapons Waste*

Articles by Patrick Oster and Bruce Ingersoll, Frank Greve, Dina Rasor, and Andrew Cockburn and Alexander Cockburn, which originally appeared in other publications, are reproduced in *More Bucks, Less Bang: How the Pentagon Buys Ineffective Weapons*, edited by Dina Rasor. The letter from Army Secretary John R. Marsh to House Defense Appropriations Subcommittee is also quoted in *More Bucks*.

CHAPTER 10 *General Dynamics*

For eighteen months, the *St. Louis Post-Dispatch* Washington Bureau investigated evidence of fraud by defense contractors. The results of these investigations by Bob Adams, Margaret Freivogel, William Freivogel, Karen Koman, and Jon Sawyer were published in the *Post-Dispatch*, December 15–22, 1985.

CHAPTER 11 *Star Wars*

George F. Kennan's warning is quoted from his 1982 article in *The New York Review of Books*. President Reagan's account of his conversation with

Premier Gorbachev is described in Eleanor Clift's December 5, 1985 article in the *Los Angeles Times*. The possible "nuclear winter" effects of space-weapon-induced fires were explored in the January 1986 issue of *Physics and Society*, on pp. 2–5. The classified R and D Associates study was reported on by Robert Scheer in the January 12, 1986, issue of the *Los Angeles Times*. John D. G. Rather's statement of the offensive potential of space-based weapons appeared in the March 7, 1985, issue of the *New York Times*.

Paul Warnke's observation about the relative strength of U.S. and Soviet forces originated in a September 29, 1981, *Los Angeles Times* interview with Robert Scheer and was quoted in *With Enough Shovels*, p. 203. Gerard Smith's comment first appeared in the June 29, 1982, issue of the *New York Times* and was quoted in *With Enough Shovels*, pp. 68–69. Scheer reported on the highly exaggerated effectiveness of "Star Wars" technology in the December 29, 1985, issue of the *Los Angeles Times*. In an article by Scheer in the *Los Angeles Times* of September 23, 1985, William Lowell Morgan criticizes his colleagues for public deception protected by classification rules. Scheer addressed the contribution of the scientific imperative toward the development of ballistic missile defense in his 1983 edition of *With Enough Shovels*, p. 289. In a December 29, 1985, article by Scheer in the *Los Angeles Times*, Col. George Hess is quoted on the inevitability of nuclear reactors in space.

The systems under consideration for ballistic missile defense were fully described and critiqued in *The Fallacy of Star Wars* by the Union of Concerned Scientists, pp. 39–152. Sidney D. Drell, Philip T. Farley, and David Holloway commented on the cost-effectiveness of producing Soviet warheads in contrast to deploying a space-based laser defense in their book *The Reagan Strategic Defense Initiative: A Technical, Political, and Arms Control Assessment*, p. 50.

General MacArthur's statement on government stampedes is taken from his speech to the stockholders of the Sperry Rand Corporation, as quoted in *A Soldier Speaks*, p. 333. Fred Hoffman is quoted in the Summer 1985 issue of *International Security*, p. 23. George A. Keyworth II justifies maintaining offensive weapons even with perfect defenses in the Fall 1984 issue of *Issues in Science and Technology*, p. 36, and was quoted in the March 1985 *Public Interest Report* by the Federation of American Scientists. James Thomson's study was outlined in his report, *Strategic Defense and Deterrence*, a May 1984 RAND Corporation publication.

Paul Nitze's rationale for a reduced offensive arsenal is from the U.S. Department of State Current Policy #751, p. 3. The Harold Brown quotation is from the March–April 1985 issue of *Survival*, p. 62. The text of the ABM Treaty and subsequent Agreed Statements are contained in *Arms Control and Disarmament Agreements: Histories of Negotiations*, a 1982 publication of the U.S. Arms Control and Disarmament Agency, pp. 139–47, 162–63.

Case by case evaluations of how the research and development status of specific weapons systems under consideration for "Star Wars" presses ABM Treaty limits were compiled by John Pike for *The Strategic Defense Initiative: Areas of Concern,* a publication of the Federation of American Scientists. The Reagan administration's handling of potential Soviet treaty violations was discussed in *Fundamentals of Nuclear Arms Control: Part IV —Treaty Compliance and Nuclear Arms Control,* a June 19, 1985, report by the U.S. House of Representatives, Foreign Affairs Committee Subcommittee on Arms Control, International Security and Science.

Paul Warnke's justification for arms control is quoted in a September 29, 1981, issue of the *Los Angeles Times* and in *With Enough Shovels,* p. 203. John Steinbruner and Edward A. Hewett are quoted in some unpublished papers prepared for the Brookings Institution in November 1981, reprinted in *With Enough Shovels,* pp. 193–95. Action-reaction patterns in U.S.-Soviet arms developments are chronologically documented in *World Military and Social Expenditures, 1985* by Ruth Leger Sivard, p. 16.

Robert S. McNamara and Hans A. Bethe's article is from the July 1985 issue of *The Atlantic Monthly,* p. 47. In an article by Robert Toth in the November 20, 1985, issue of the *Los Angeles Times,* Robert McFarlane acknowledged the danger of weapons that can escape detection. The reaction of the Reagan administration to the existence of Soviet strategic defense activities was quoted from the U.S. Department of Defense and Department of State document, *Soviet Strategic Defense Programs,* October 1985, p. 21.

Bibliography

BOOKS

Adams, Gordon. *The Politics of Defense Contracting: The Iron Triangle.* New Brunswick: Transaction Books, 1982.

Alperovitz, Gar. *Atomic Diplomacy: Hiroshima and Potsdam, The Use of the Atomic Bomb and the American Confrontation with Soviet Power.* New York: Simon and Schuster, 1965.

Ambrose, Stephen E. *Eisenhower the President.* New York: Simon and Schuster, 1984.

Barash, David P., and Judith Eve Lipton. *The Caveman and the Bomb: Human Nature, Evolution, and Nuclear War.* New York: McGraw-Hill, 1985.

Broad, William J. *Star Warriors.* New York: Simon and Schuster, 1985.

Carter, Ashton B., and David N. Schwartz, eds. *Ballistic Missile Defense.* Washington, D.C.: The Brookings Institution, 1984.

Collier, Basil. *Arms and the Men.* London: Hamish Hamilton, 1979.

Craven, W. F., and J. L. Cate. *The Army Air Forces in World War II.* Vol. 5. Chicago: University of Chicago Press, 1953.

Donovan, Robert J. *Conflict and Crisis: the Presidency of Harry S. Truman, 1945–1948.* New York: W. W. Norton & Co., Inc., 1977.

Drell, Sidney D., Philip J. Farley, and David Holloway. *The Reagan Strategic Defense Initiative: A Technical, Political, and Arms Control Assessment.* Cambridge, Mass.: Ballinger Publishing Co., 1985.

Eisenhower, Dwight D. *Crusade in Europe.* Garden City, N.Y.: Doubleday, 1948.

———. *Mandate for Change, 1953–1956.* Garden City, N.Y.: Doubleday, 1963.

Engelbrecht, H. C. and F. C. Hanighen. *Merchants of Death.* New York: Dodd, Mead, 1934.

Fallows, James. *National Defense.* New York: Vintage Books, 1981.

Ferrell, Robert H., ed. *Off the Record: The Private Papers of Harry S. Truman.* New York: Harper & Row, 1980.

Ferrero, Guglielmo. *The Principles of Power: The Great Political Crisis of History.* New York: G. P. Putnam's Sons, 1942.

Fulbright, William. *The Pentagon Propaganda Machine.* New York: Liveright, 1970.

Gansler, Jacques S. *The Defense Industry.* Cambridge, Mass.: MIT Press, 1984.

Klare, Michael T. *American Arms Supermarket.* Austin: University of Texas Press, 1984.

Kurzman, Dan. *Day of the Bomb: Countdown to Hiroshima.* New York: McGraw-Hill, 1986.

Lamont, Lansing. *Day of Trinity.* New York: Atheneum, 1965.

Leahy, William D. *I Was There.* New York: Whittlesey House, 1950.

Noel-Baker, Philip. *The Private Manufacture of Arms.* New York: Oxford University Press, 1937.

———. *The Arms Race.* Dobbs Ferry, N.Y.: Oceana Publications, 1958.

Pringle, Peter, and William Arkin. *S.I.O.P.: The Secret U.S. Plan for Nuclear War.* New York: W. W. Norton & Co., 1983.

Rasor, Dina, ed. *More Bucks, Less Bang: How the Pentagon Buys Ineffective Weapons.* Washington, D.C.: Fund for Constitutional Government, 1983.

———. *The Pentagon Underground: Hidden Patriots Fighting Against Deceit and Fraud in America's Defense Program.* New York: Times Books, 1985.

Seldes, George. *Iron, Blood and Profits: An Exposure of the World-Wide Munitions Racket.* New York: Harper Brothers, 1934.

Terkel, Studs. *The Good War: An Oral History of World War II.* New York: Pantheon Books, 1984.

Wahn, Vorin W., Jr. ed. *A Soldier Speaks.* New York: Praeger, 1965.

Wiltz, John E. *In Search of Peace: The Senate Munitions Inquiry, 1934–36.* Baton Rouge: Louisiana State University Press, 1963.

Wyden, Peter. *Day One: Before Hiroshima and After.* New York: Simon and Schuster, 1984.

MAGAZINE ARTICLES, NEWSPAPER ARTICLES, PAMPHLETS

Adams, Bob, and Margaret Freivogel, William Freivogel, Karen Koman, Jon Sawyer. "Lines of Defense: Tracking Pentagon Waste," *St. Louis Post-Dispatch.* March to December 1985.

Anthan, George. "The Pentagon Shivers When CDI Speaks: Respected Watchdog Group Gets Cool to Military Waste," *The Des Moines Register.* November 26, 1976.

Baber, Asa. "What You're Not Supposed to Know About the Arms Race," *Playboy.* June 1981.

Belay, William. "The $13 Billion Dud," *California Magazine.* February 1983.

Boffey, Philip M. "Dark Side of 'Star Wars': System Could Also Attack," *New York Times.* March 7, 1985.

Brown, Harold. "The Strategic Defense Initiative: Defensive Systems and the Strategic Debate," *Survival.* March–April 1985.

Clift, Eleanor. "Space Invaders Would Unite U.S. and Soviets, Reagan Says," *Los Angeles Times.* December 5, 1985.

Cockburn, Andrew, and Alexander Cockburn. "The Myth of Missile Accuracy," *New York Review of Books.* November 20, 1980.

Cousins, Norman, and Thomas K. Finletter. "A Beginning for Sanity," *The Saturday Review of Literature.* June 15, 1946.

Duscha, Julius. "Power on the Potomac," *The Washingtonian.* January 1973.

Fallows, James. "M-16: A Bureaucratic Horror Story," *Atlantic Monthly.* June 1981.

Fitzgerald, A. Ernest. "The Pentagon as the Enemy of Capitalism," *World Magazine.* February 27, 1973.

Fritz, Sara. "Conferees Bar Anti-Satellite Weapons Test," *Los Angeles Times.* December 14, 1985.

Greve, Frank. "Dream Weapon a Nightmare," *Knight-Ridder Newspapers.* May 2, 1982.

———. "Pershing 2 Missile: Does The Thing Work?" *Knight-Ridder Newspapers.* June 21, 1982.

Hersenberg, Caroline L. "Nuclear Winter and Strategic Defense Initiative," *Physics and Society.* January 1986.

Hoffman, Fred S. "The SDI in U.S. Nuclear Strategy," *International Security.* Summer 1985.

Kennan, George F. "On Nuclear War," *The New York Review of Books.* January 21, 1982.

Keyworth, George A. II. "The Case for Strategic Defense: An Option for a World Disarmed," *Issues in Science and Technology.* Fall 1984.

Knickerbocker, Brad. "Former US Admiral Challenges Basis of Military Thinking," *The Christian Science Monitor.* October 30, 1984.

Krepon, Michael. "Arms Control: Verification and Compliance," *Foreign Policy Association.* Fall 1984.

McNamara, Robert S., and Hans A. Bethe. "Reducing the Risk of Nuclear War," *The Atlantic Monthly.* July 1985.

Oster, Patrick, and Bruce Ingersoll. "M-1," *Chicago Sun-Times.* April 16, 1981.

Pierson, John. "A Weather Eye on the Military," *The Wall Street Journal.* April 24, 1972.

Pike, John. "The Strategic Defense Initiative: Areas of Concern," Federation of American Scientists. June 10, 1985.

——— and Jonathan Rich. "Public Interest Report," Federation of American Scientists. March 1984.

Rasor, Dina. "Fighting with Failures," *Reason.* April 1982.

Royce, Knut. "Stealth Bomber Called 'a Joke' " and "Huge Stealth Bomber was a Modest Idea," *Hearst Newspapers.* December 5–6, 1982.

Scheer, Robert. " 'Star Wars': A Program in Disarray," *Los Angeles Times.* September 22, 1985.

———. "Flaws Peril Pivotal 'Star Wars' Laser," *Los Angeles Times.* September 23, 1985.

———. "Scientists Split Over 'Star Wars,' " *Los Angeles Times.* September 24, 1985.

———. " 'Star Wars': All-out Push to Gain Funding," *Los Angeles Times.* December 29, 1985.

———. " 'Star Wars' Lasers Held Able to Incinerate Cities," *Los Angeles Times.* January 12, 1986.

Schlesinger, James R. "Rhetoric and Realities in the Star Wars Debate," *International Security.* Summer 1985.

Thomson, James. "Strategic Defense and Deterrence," The RAND Corporation. May 1984.

Tirman, John, ed. *The Fallacy of Star Wars,* Union of Concerned Scientists. New York: Vintage Books, October 1984.

Toth, Robert C. "Technology Defies Arms Control Effort," *Los Angeles Times.* November 20, 1985.

"Was A-Bomb on Japan a Mistake?" *U.S. News and World Report* interviews with James F. Byrnes and others. August 15, 1960.

GOVERNMENT PUBLICATIONS

President's Blue Ribbon Commission on Defense Management, David Pac-
kard, Chairman. *An Interim Report to The President.* February 1986.
————. *A Formula for Action.* April 1986.
————. *Conduct and Accountability.* June 1986.
U.S. Arms Control and Disarmament Agency, *Arms Control and Disarma-
ment Agreements: Histories of Negotiations.* 1982.
U.S. Arms Control and Disarmament Agency, *World Military Expenditures
and Arms Transfers.* 1985.
U.S. Department of State, Bureau of Public Affairs, Paul H. Nitze. *SDI: Its
Nature and Rationale,* Current Policy #751.
U.S. Department of Defense, *The Entry of the Soviet Union into the War
Against Japan: Military Plans, 1941–1945.* 1955.
U.S. Department of Defense and Department of State, *Soviet Strategic
Defense Programs.* October 1985.
U.S. Strategic Bombing Survey, *Japan's Struggle to End the War.* 1946.
U.S. House of Representatives Armed Services Committee Subcommittee
on Seapower and Strategic and Critical Materials, and Subcommittee
on Investigations, joint hearings, *Review of Allowable Costs in Overhead
Submission of Defense Contractors.* 1985.
U.S. House of Representatives, Committee on Armed Services, Hearings
before the Subcommittee on the M-16 Rifle Program. 1967.
U.S. House of Representatives Foreign Affairs Committee Subcommittee on
Arms Control, International Security and Science, *Fundamentals of
Nuclear Arms Control: Part IV—Treaty Compliance and Nuclear Arms
Control.* June 19, 1985.
U.S. Senate, Special Committee Investigating the Munitions Industry. 1934.

Index